BURNING PASSIONS

Burning Passions

An Introduction to the Study of Silent Cinema

Paolo Cherchi Usai

PREFACE BY KEVIN BROWNLOW

TRANSLATED BY EMMA SANSONE RITTLE

BRITISH FILM INSTITUTE

bfi

BFI PUBLISHING

First published in 1994 by the
British Film Institute
21 Stephen Street
London W1P 1PL

Reprinted 1995

The British Film Institute exists to encourage the development of film, television and
video in the United Kingdom, and to promote knowledge, understanding and
enjoyment of the culture of the moving image. Its activities include the National Film
and Television Archive; the National Film Theatre; the Museum of the Moving
Image; the London Film Festival; the production and distribution of film and video;
funding and support for regional activities; Library and Information Services; Stills,
Posters and Design; Research, Publishing and Education; and the monthly *Sight and
Sound* magazine.

British Library Cataloguing in Publication Data
A catalogue record for this book is available from the British Library

ISBN 0–85170–407–7
      0–85170–408–5 pbk

Cover by Design & Art
Cover photograph: *The Vampire* (Robert Vignola, 1913)

Typesetting by Fakenham Photosetting Ltd, Fakenham, Norfolk
Printed in Great Britain by The Trinity Press, Worcester

CONTENTS

LIST OF PLATES

Plates Illustrating Format (between pages 74 and 79)

1 Lumière, 35mm, 1895–1900
2 Demenÿ, 60mm, 1896
3 Veriscope, 63mm, 1897
4 Duplex, 11mm, 1915–27
5 Edison Home Kinetoscope, 22mm
6 Ernemann Kino, 17.5mm, 1903
7 Duoscope, 17.5mm, 1912
8 Kino-Salon, 35mm, 1908–9
9 American Mutoscope & Biograph, 70mm, 1903
10 American Mutoscope & Biograph, 70mm, 1895–1905
11 Filoteo Alberini, 70mm, 1911
12 Pathé-Kok, 28mm, 1912
13 Cine Kodak, 16mm, 1920
14 Paper print, 35mm, *c*. 1912
15 Chrono de Poche, 15mm, 1900
16 Movette, 17.5mm, 1917
17 Pathé-baby or Pathex, 9.5mm, 1922–3
18 35mm print, 1905–6
19 35mm print, *c*. 1904
20 Casimir Sivan, 35mm, *c*. 1896
21 Max Skladanowsky, 55mm, 1895
22 35mm print, 1920
23 Cement splice on 35mm positive, 1899
24 Cement splice on 35mm negative, 1899
25 Charles Urban, Spirograph, 1923
26 Charles Urban Spirograph, 1923, detail
27 L. U. Kamm, Kammatograph, 1898–1900
28 L. U. Kamm, Kammatograph, 1898–1900, detail
29 Technicolor process no. 2, 1926
30 Lumière, 75mm, 1900

Plates Illustrating Colour (between pages 86 and 87)

NOTE TO THE ENGLISH EDITION

In the spring of 1989 Edoardo Pia, editorial director of the Turin publishing company UTET, suggested that I should write a spectator's guide to the silent cinema. He knew of my interest in the subject because in 1986 he had published my anthology on Giovanni Pastrone, the director of the epic film *Cabiria* (1914). Edoardo Pia had the courage to publish a book which was not organised on rigorously academic lines and which dealt with a subject that, at least in Italy, had received only sporadic attention in a strictly scholarly context. For this I owe him a debt of gratitude.

At first, *Burning Passions* was the title of a lecture at the Cineteca di Bologna in December 1988. In 1991, UTET first published my *Una passione infiammabile* and I hoped originally that the book would find a readership among Italian students, researchers and archivists. I therefore devoted almost an entire chapter to the Italian film archives. For the English version of the book, this chapter has been completely recast in an international perspective. I have also modified, integrated and corrected other parts of the text following many suggestions which reached me while I was in San Culebra del Porco, where the quietly stimulating atmosphere helped transform the tedium of rewriting a book into a gratifying and in some ways fascinating experience.

Particularly helpful were the correspondence and the conversations with Clyde Jeavons and Anne Fleming, respectively Curator and Deputy Curator of the National Film and Television Archive in London; Geoffrey Nowell-Smith; Jan-Christopher Horak, Edward E. Stratmann, Robin Blair Bolger, Becky Simmons and the staff of the Film Department of the International Museum of Photography and Film at George Eastman House, Rochester, New York; Paul C. Spehr and Pat Loughney at the Motion Picture, Broadcasting and Recorded Sound Division, Library of Congress, Washington, DC; Bo Berglund (Malmö, Sweden); Jonathan Dennis (Wellington, New Zealand); Ann Baylis (National Film and Sound Archive, Canberra, Australia); Ben Brewster (Wisconsin Center for Film and Theater Research, Madison, Wis.); Susan Dalton (American Film Institute, Washington, DC); Roger Smither (Film Department, Imperial War Museum, London); Brigitte van der Elst (Fédération Internationale des Archives du Film, Brussels); Kristin Thompson (University of Wisconsin, Madison); and especially Roland Cosandey (Vevey, Switzerland), whose perceptive notes, beginning with the title 'Une passion inflammable (et transmissible)', encouraged my belief in the potential value of this project.

PAOLO CHERCHI USAI
Canberra, January 1993

PREFACE

KEVIN BROWNLOW

Poor silent films! Can any art have been treated so shabbily? Even those who respect the films often treat them with such reverence – projecting them too slow, without music – that the life is squeezed out of them. Those who don't respect them have a record of destruction worthy of Attila the Hun: they have burned them, dumped them in the sea, hacked the reels with axes, or let them rot in the vaults.

From the moment sound arrived, it was commercially useful to dispel the magic of the silent film; they were derided in print and on the screen as ludicrous, technically inept and badly acted. Something merely to be laughed at. People of my generation will remember Biographs of the 1910–12 period, in appalling prints, much speeded up, with 'humorous' commentaries, shown among the cartoons at news theatres in the 1940s and 1950s.

The propaganda worked. Ask anyone in their seventies and eighties about silent films, and the enthusiasm will be clouded by apology. 'They all moved very fast.'

Some of them undoubtedly did. Projectionists liked to get home, and the more unscrupulous would sometimes 'race' the film – increasing the pace far beyond the speed appropriate for it. They could do that because motors had rheostats, unlike today, when projectors are fixed at a standard speed of 24 frames per second. There was no standard speed in the silent days. D. W. Griffith's Biographs were shot at anything from 14 to 18 frames a second, but 16 was the average. Over at the Edison studio, at the same time, they shot much faster. Projectionists must have become very confused.

By the 1920s when the pit piano had often been replaced by a pit orchestra, it was essential for musicians and projectionists to know the speed, and cue sheets were issued. They make instructive reading. The 'average' speed was around 20–22 f.p.s., and sometimes 24. I doubt whether any cameraman cranked at 24, but that wasn't the point; the films were shown slightly faster than they were shot. When sound arrived, and everything settled down to the speed at which the films were photographed, audiences complained of a 'slow motion' effect. And now, when *Wings* (1927) is shown by a film society at the

1

so-called silent speed of 16 f.p.s., it lasts an hour longer than it did on its original release.

Yet it would be fair to say that in most cinemas in the 1920s you saw original prints, decently presented at a reasonable speed, which is more than one could hope for today.

Worse than the speed problem is the question of prints. Make no mistake, the standard of photography in the silent days was remarkably high. The cameramen had the tradition of Victorian still photographers to draw upon and even the least pretentious film could boast superb cinematography. Seen in a nitrate print projected on a big screen, the best work of the silent era can be an overwhelming artistic experience. Copy it, and at once the magic disappears. It is like copying a Rembrandt with an Instamatic camera. The silver content of black-and-white film stock has been removed to such an extent that the glistening sheen of early cinematography often registers as an out-of-focus smear. The information is there. The art has gone.

Once, any laboratory could make serviceable black-and-white prints. Now, apart from the specialists, none of them can. The men who knew how to cope with black and white have long since retired and few of their replacements have any skill beyond their daily concern with colour film. Ask them to print black and white on colour stock, and you will need a remarkably patient and sensitive technician to work with you.

What else has a silent film apart from its visuals? Its subtitles – or intertitles, as they are now called – convey plot and dialogue points. Everything else comes from the image. Degrade that even slightly and you are removing essential information. How often have you seen a print of a silent film in which the actors faces register as a white blob? Without the benefit of those expressions – which were often very subtle – you have not seen those performances, or, for that matter, that film.

I remember watching a rare film during a Garbo season at a London cinema. It was a beautiful print, but shown out of focus. I asked an usher to contact the projectionist. 'Nothing you can do about that,' said the usher. 'It's an old film, you're lucky to see anything.'

As a film collector, I have had to give up acquiring new prints of silent films, because the results simply depress me. I am old enough to have seen silents in their original nitrate form, shown during the 1950s and 60s, and I have never forgotten the impact of the razor-sharp exteriors, the gauzed close-ups, the ravishing use of tints and tones, and the sheer depth of the image. They say depth of focus was invented for *Citizen Kane*; take a look at a few silent pictures! (They say ceilings first appeared in *Kane*, too, and, as much as I revere *Kane*, a forgotten historical epic of 1924 called *Lady of Quality* made a feature of showing astoundingly elaborate Tudor ceilings on all its interior sets.)

Whenever my wife and I find ourselves in the country on a day when the light is immaculate, she invariably says, 'What wonderful nitrate weather!' She is not a specialist, but she refuses to watch silent films on video, and I cannot blame her. Video is a wonderful medium; it releases you from the tyranny of the programme controllers, and it makes films as cheap and as widely available as paperback books. But while the impact of, say, Dickens is as powerful in paperback as in the finest binding, the effect of a silent film is disastrously diminished. The photographic quality undergoes severe degradation, even if the transfer is made from the finest prints. In America, the old-fashioned NTSC softens the definition and flattens the contrast and often produces a double-image. Laserdisc can be an improvement, but all too often transfers to disc are made from videotape rather than film.

With video, you are at the mercy of those who make the transfer for what speed you get. And what grading you get. And how much of the picture you see. One company in America puts out Buster Keaton's *The General* (1927) at the so-called silent speed of 16 f.p.s., even though Buster Keaton wanted it shown at 24. When I wrote to ask why they had committed such an unnecessary sin, they said they had made a close study of the movement within the film – including the smoke (!) – and had come to a corporate decision; it looked better at 16. It also added the equivalent of four reels to the running time. Keaton's comedy can survive almost everything – even terrible prints – but it cannot survive a deadly pace. Anyone watching that particular video could be forgiven for dismissing silent comedy as unbearably slow.

The opposite is equally awful – when you buy a video of D. W. Griffith's *Intolerance* (1916) to discover that it has been transferred at 24 f.p.s. The cameras on *Intolerance* turned at 16 and 18 f.p.s. and to increase the speed transforms Griffith's epic drama into farce. One of the drawbacks with video – which should be a strength – is that once the speed is set there is no way of altering it.

Why is it that the combined efforts of specialised film and video distributors make the technicians responsible for the old films look like idiots? The sad fact is that the public don't blame the people who made the print – they blame the age of the film, and those who produced it.

Archives are sometimes guilty as well. Some have done magnificent work over the years. Others have merely served as tombs for decomposing nitrate. How many of us mourned when we saw at Pordenone Lois Weber's remarkably realistic drama *Shoes* (1916), surviving in a copy savaged by the marks of bad storage and decomposition? Had it been kept by some eccentric collector in a hen house? No, it was preserved by one of the world's leading archives, by an old regime concerned only with copying films of its own nationality. The new broom has swept away that destructive idea and it rescued *Shoes* – albeit in a fragile and fragmentary state – just before it finally gave up the ghost.

Fortunately, there is good news in all this. A new generation of silent film enthusiasts are achieving miracles. Pordenone holds a festival of silent films – Le Giornate del Cinema Muto – once a year, the only place in the world that does so. Pordenone has a long list of achievements to its credit, and the fact that at last there is a place where silent films are regularly shown has encouraged archives to make more rarities available. Pordenone aims at showing the best available prints, but sometimes the heads of the archives are present to witness the cultural crimes committed by their predecessors: murky and incomplete copies. Pordenone always provides live music, either a piano, or, when they can afford it, a full orchestra.

Silent films are high on the agenda of Bologna (Il Cinema Ritrovato) and Paris (CinéMémoire), both of which were inspired by the example of Pordenone. More and more silent films are being restored, and no one who saw them will forget Renée Lichtig's restoration of Volkoff's *Casanova* (1926) for the Cinémathèque Française, or Bob Gitt's of Chester Franklin's *Toll of the Sea* (1922), the first successful Technicolor feature, for UCLA Film Archives.

Paolo Cherchi Usai has been in the vanguard of all this activity as one of the founders of Pordenone. With the indomitable Pordenone team, he has opened our eyes to aspects of the silent era we never dreamed existed. To achieve this he has had to immerse himself in archives all over the world. Recently, he has been working full-time at George Eastman House, in Rochester, NY. I have often wished that a book could be written about the problems of researching silent film, and the problems of dealing with archives. Paolo Cherchi Usai has written that book.

Introduction

Ah! les cow-boys du muet, les vampires du tacite, les maxlinder du silen-
cieux, les charlot de l'aphone, combien passionné fus-je de leur geste, épique
en son genre, dirais-je.

Raymond Queneau

This book is intended as a researcher's guide to the moving photographic
images produced during the so-called 'silent period'. Normally, this definition
covers the years 1895 to 1927, between the patenting of the Cinématographe
Lumière and the first public projection of Alan Crosland's *The Jazz Singer*,
which included some sung and spoken sequences. Despite their immense
significance, these two events are insufficient to define the area of research into
which we shall venture.

Photographs shown in quick succession to achieve the effect of movement were already known to the public from the year before the first screening
of *La Sortie des usines Lumière*. To form an idea of the technological and the
creative antecedents of that event, we must go back at least to 1893 and even
further, to the embryonic machines for the reproduction of animated images
on light-sensitive material. These machines allowed a single spectator to see
sequences lasting a handful of seconds: but they *were* photographic sequences
on paper or film, not drawings or painted glass slides.

Later, many of these scenes were made available for collective viewing,
and some of the ones that survived can now be consulted in film archives,
although no longer in their original form. That such scenes saw the light of
day on dates which do not coincide with those of Edison's first public demon-
strations or with the famous evening in Paris on 28 December 1895 at the
Grand Café, does not seem to me to be sufficient reason to neglect them. I
think that all who are concerned with pre-cinema will agree that chronological
divisions are more arbitrary than demarcations between adjacent disciplines
according to their research methods.

At the opposite end of the era of the praxinoscope is the long twilight of
the silent film. This began with experiments to record sound directly onto film
(much earlier than 1927: the first studies on the subject were published in 1901)
and ended only around 1935, almost a decade after the official beginning of
sound films. It is true that in 1930 silent cinema was considered an anachro-
nism in Western Europe and in the United States. However, one must bear in
mind that any alignment with such a radical technological innovation had to

cope with many hesitations and delays: *La canzone dell'amore*, the first Italian sound film, was shown on 7 October 1930; the Soviet Union continued to produce silent films until 1935; the last surviving Chinese silent film, *Mitu de gaoyang*, dates from 1936.

Besides, the presence or absence of a soundtrack on a print is not enough to establish the historical identity of a silent film. Experimental cinema has been, and sometimes still is, devoid of sound, but that does not mean it can be equated with the silent cinema of the early days. The same can be said of some pornographic productions. In contrast, Victor Sjöström's *The Wind* (1928), which was distributed in a version with synchronised sound after the production company had delayed its release, belongs firmly to the aesthetics of silent cinema and is unanimously regarded as one of its most fully realised results.

Even if we must take into account the 'sound film' experiments made in the period under consideration, the 'silent film' mentioned in the first chapters of the histories of cinema and which will be described in the following pages is in fact the cinema produced and distributed during the years when the only means of providing sound was to make the moment of projection coincide with the use of mechanical equipment outside the film, with the performance of live music, and with the direct intervention of barkers, singers and actors in front of or beside the screen. All three techniques were used, systematically or on specific occasions, throughout the existence of 'silent cinema'.

But then, if the spectators at the time were hardly ever surrounded by silence, why insist on calling it 'silent'? Perhaps we should look more deeply to differentiate between ways of organising visual meaning. Some scholars have claimed, for example, that cinema underwent a structural transformation – in productive, stylistic and technological terms – between 1911 and 1917, long before 'sound' appeared on the horizon. Their arguments are often well founded, and there is no doubt that the distinction between silent and sound cinema has lost the rigour which general usage still tends to attribute to it.

However, there are still many excellent reasons for continuing to speak and to write of 'silent cinema' in its familiar usage, and for interpreting it as such. Some are to do with the present volume's *raison d'être*. But first I would like to remind the reader of the reasons pertaining to the times when silent cinema was a daily entertainment for millions of spectators. To begin with, cinema in the early 20th century was *aware* of being silent and defined itself as such in the certainty that this aspect was the essential component of a new art form. This certainty was accompanied by the belief (or fear) that its primitive condition was destined to end, sooner or later. Headlines in trade magazines and periodicals used the term 'silent', often in order to free cinema from theatre and literature. The shrewder producers and directors identified cinema's possibilities with the concepts of vision and gesture, and considered the absence of sound (despite the musicians and actors in the cinema hall) a defining fact rather than a limitation.

The second observation directly follows from the first. The change from 'silent' to 'sound' cinema (in the above-mentioned meaning) was more than a technological revolution: it threw the film industry into a period of turbulent transition affecting tens of thousands of people who suddenly found themselves out of work, who had to adapt to the new reality or who owed their success to this reality. Together with their destiny, the spectators changed too as their way of perceiving reproduced visual artefacts changed. From being an art of abstraction, displaying a problematic coexistence between the image (the shot) and the written word (the intertitle), cinema became the mouthpiece of an ambiguous, subtle mimesis, which could redefine and shape the nature of the collective imagination.

The abruptness of such a change moved silent cinema away from the sensibility of spectators living in the latter part of the 20th century and caused its decline. Since then, silent film has become the object of archaeological study and only rarely of public entertainment: not because the moving pictures of the first thirty years were technically backward, but because they seemed to belong to an extinct tradition which most people could no longer decipher.

This book aims to provide useful tools to understand this tradition and to fight the prejudices surrounding it (including its status as a dead language) through the study of documents whose primary characteristics are that they are extremely perishable and changeable. Although it is designed as an introduction, the reader already familar with the subject may find here a useful reminder of concepts, technical data and debates in the field. Like all manuals, this one contains information and advice which may appear pedantic but without which the encounter with silent cinema becomes merely a superficial and, at best, a nostalgic exercise. In this respect, the book is certainly not meant to be used as a manual for film criticism or as a source of ideas for public screenings as practised by festivals and film archives. Neither is it, however, a set of instructions for establishing or joining an intellectual sect. The admittedly more ambitious purpose of this guide is quite the opposite.

We can summarise it with a metaphor: the original copies of silent films, apart from being perishable, are highly flammable. This peculiarity symbolises the aesthetic pleasure which examining a film from the silent period can bring to a careful but not disenchanted eye. Learning to watch silent films means trying to identify with a lost visual sensitivity. It also means going back to the origins of a truly inflammable, even explosive relationship between image and mind, provided that this relationship is cultivated with the rigour of the historian and the imagination of a spectator aware of reliving another's past in a beam of light projected onto a screen.

This is why in this book films are at the centre of our attention, and written sources, even though it is impossible to reconstruct the cinema's past without them, take second place. Ways of researching in libraries and in specialised magazines, which will be mentioned briefly, are familiar to anyone who knows the rules of intellectual work. Gaining access to the actual moving images, and knowing how to interpret them, requires other efforts and other rules, which I have tried to summarise here.

Eileen Bowser, Harold Brown, Kevin Brownlow, David Francis, Angelo R. Humouda, Jacques L'Aumône, Enno Patalas, Vincent Pinel, the late George C. Pratt, Martin Sopocy and Davide Turconi have helped me to learn and apply these rules, although the responsibility for any omissions or inaccuracies in describing them will be mine alone. My wife Daniela has verified them in the light of a deeper and more intimately burning passion, which has irradiated silent cinema and all areas beyond.

Rochester, New York
September 1990

1

WHAT IS A SILENT FILM?

I want to see this Annie Mattygraph. What time does she come on?
Cartoon caption, *Scraps* (London), 16 January 1897

The Base

Motion-picture film stock manufactured at the time of silent cinema consists almost entirely of highly unstable organic materials. Some photographically obtained moving images were printed on supports other than film: the Kammatograph (1898–1900), for instance, uses a glass disc with about 400 frames arranged in a spiral (see Plates 27 and 28; a similar technique was adopted for Charles Urban's Spirograph, which used a flexible disc, Plates 25 and 26); the mutoscope is a cylinder holding several hundred rectangles of paper (see Plate 9), each of them bearing a photograph so that, if observed in rapid sequence through equipment for individual viewing, an impression of continuous movement is generated. The same effect is obtained through the Théoscope, produced in France by Théophile Lacroix according to a principle similar to that of the American model.

However, from the end of the 19th century, cellulose film established itself as the preferred material for the reproduction of moving images. Its components remained essentially unchanged for several decades: a base; a very thin gelatin adhesive layer; a light-sensitive emulsion – recognisable as the opaque side of the film – connected to the base by the adhesive layer, and normally consisting of a suspension of silver salts in gelatin. There are sometimes two additional layers: a thin gelatin layer, protecting the emulsion from mechanical damage caused by the use of the film, and a further layer to prevent a haze from forming on the image, or to prevent the film from curling.

The base of most films produced up to February 1951 is cellulose nitrate, a highly flammable substance; from then on, nitrate was replaced by cellulose acetate – which is much less flammable – and in some cases by polyester. From the first decade of the 20th century, however, some companies were already experimenting with the production of so-called safety films, in cellulose acetate (this invention by Eichengrun and Becker dates from 1901) or in nitrate covered by non-flammable substances (the first known examples of this film stock date from 1909).

Formats

The commercial development of cinema dates from the production of film – with perforations on either side of the frame so that it may be mechanically pulled through the projector – printed on a 35mm-wide flexible base developed in 1889 by Henry M. Reichenbach for George Eastman from an invention attributed to, among others, the brothers J. W. and I. S. Hyatt (1865), Hannibal Goodwin (1888) and Reichenbach himself. This was the format which Thomas Edison adopted for his Kinetoscope, a device allowing one spectator at a time to see brief strips of film. The Kinetoscope was so successful commercially that subsequent machines for the reproduction of moving images adopted 35mm as a standard format. This tendency was also encouraged by the Eastman company: their film for still picture cameras was 70mm wide. This meant they could simply cut the film in half lengthways to obtain a motion picture film-base of the desired size. The success of the cinema as a form of mass entertainment is tied to this type of film, officially adopted by all production companies in 1909.

The mechanics of Edison's Kinetoscope also determined the use of 35mm film with four vaguely rectangular perforations on either side of each frame. Other inventors, at the end of the 19th century, resorted to different types of perforation. The one most commonly used prior to Edison's design was that by the Lumière brothers: the film is drawn along by means of one single, circular perforation on either side of the frame (see Plate 1). Other more short-lived systems were designed by Max Skladanowsky in Germany (three circular perforations on each side, two of them corresponding to the frame line, as in Plate 21; later, four perforations on both sides of the frame, as in the Edison system, but much smaller and also circular) and by the British company Prestwich (three circular perforations on each side of the frame).

The size and shape of Edison's perforations remained substantially unchanged – although with considerable differences according to the perforating machine used – until 1905 (Plate 19). From 1905 to 1924 the perforations of negative and positive films became larger, and their shape was redesigned as rectangles with slightly rounded sides (Plate 22). In 1924, a further change was introduced with two different types of perforations: the Kodak standard for positive film and the Bell & Howell for negative film. The aim was to adapt the print to the different kinds of mechanical stresses during shooting and repeated projection. A proposal was made to unify the two kinds of perforation (Dubray-Howell system), but it met with little favour.

From 1895 to 1916, especially in the United States, a record was kept of the images printed on 35mm film: the images were reprinted on strips of photographic paper, often including the perforations (paper prints: Plate 14). Clearly, these 'films' cannot be screened; each frame, however, can be reproduced on photographic film with good results. Many early American films are currently available only on copies obtained from these paper prints, deposited by the producers in order to obtain legal protection against possible forgeries.

Non-Standard Formats

In spite of its success, there are alternatives to, and rivals of, the 35mm format, as well as famous victims.

The American Mutoscope & Biograph Company, active between the end of the 19th century and the beginning of the 20th century, produced mutoscope films. They used 70mm film without lateral perforations. The ratio between height and width of the frame (the aspect ratio) is about 3:4; as there are no perforations, the image takes up almost the whole width of the film (Plates 9 and 10). The resulting picture projected on the screen was substantially sharper than that of the standard 35mm image, which contributed to the company's success.

From 1896 onwards, some 60mm films were made. A 60mm Prestwich film, with four perforations along the edges of the frame and an aspect ratio similar to the 35mm image format, is preserved in the National Film and Television Archive in London. The 60mm film by the Frenchman Georges Demenÿ (Plate 2) has fifteen perforations every four frames.

In 1897, the American Veriscope Company made a 63mm film of which only one specimen is known: *The Corbett–Fitzsimmons Fight*, the chronicle of a boxing match (Plate 3). The Veriscope format has five perforations per frame on each side; the aspect ratio of the frame is 1:1.75.

The 75mm format (with a frame 45mm high and 60mm wide) was suggested, as an experiment, by Louis Lumière in 1898 (Plate 30).

Two years later, in 1900, Gaumont distributed the *Chrono de poche*, a portable motion-picture camera which used 15mm film with central perforations (Plate 15).

In 1902, the Warwick Trading Company introduced a 17.5mm film for amateur use in the Biokam, a machine which could shoot, print and project film. Here, too, there is only one perforation, on the frame line; this idea was taken up by Ernemann in Germany (with a different shaped perforation: Plate 6) and by Pathé in the 1920s, among others.

After the 70mm film stock used by the American Mutoscope & Biograph, the next alternative format to 35mm that met with a degree of success (perhaps because its frame is only slightly smaller than that of 35mm film) was the 28mm film introduced by Pathé in 1912 as the Pathé-Kok brand. A characteristic of this film, printed on a non-flammable (safety) base starting from nitrate negatives, is the asymmetric perforation system: three perforations per frame on one side, one perforation per frame on the opposite side (Plate 12). In the copies printed in the United States (Pathescope), there are three perforations on each side.

The amateur film par excellence, 16mm, was invented by Eastman Kodak in 1920; the first version of this format, known as Kodascope, used 'reversal' positive film: it could be taken directly from the camera and transformed into a positive copy which could be screened straight away. Almost all film in this format was produced on safety stock (Plate 13).

In 1923, Pathé launched another amateur format, 9.5mm (Pathé-baby), a strong competitor with 16mm for some years. Positive copies in 9.5mm were made on non-flammable film (Plate 17).

Different producers thought up even more unusual formats, until they reached bizarre extremes. For instance, Itala Film of Turin tried a 35mm frame divided into four parts to accommodate four different shots. There was Edison's 22mm film (Home Kinetoscope) with three strips of frames just over 5mm wide, each strip divided by a line of perforations (Plate 5). The German firm Messter's Kino-Salon had four series of frames and three lines of perforations on a film just under 35mm wide (Plate 8). Oko film by the Pole Kazimierz Prószynski (1913) was a 120mm film divided into rows of 15 frames. None of these systems (with the partial exception of the Home Kinetoscope) went past the experimental stage or achieved wide sales. The often unique images recorded on these 'monsters' of technology are in danger of disappearing sooner than the others, because the machines needed to project them are extremely rare and it is difficult and expensive to transfer them onto more familiar formats.

Colour

The black-and-white film commonly used until the mid-1920s, called orthochromatic film, was sensitive to ultra-violet, violet and blue light, and partially sensitive to yellow and green radiations, while red had no effect on the silver bromide emulsion. In order to prevent certain objects appearing on the screen as indistinct dark stains, the technicians constantly had to monitor the colour balance on the sets, avoiding certain colours for costumes and even painting backgrounds in various shades of grey for interior shots. Orthochromatic film remained in use until the early 1940s, mainly for special effects and for the blue strip in the 3-strip Technicolor process after the late 1920s.

Panchromatic film, developed at the end of 1912 by the Eastman Kodak Company on behalf of Gaumont, was sensitive to almost the entire spectrum of visible radiation. At first, it was used only sporadically, partly because it was expensive. However, within a four-year period (from 1922 – the year of Ned Van Buren's *The Headless Horseman*, the first full-length feature shot entirely on a panchromatic negative – to 1926), panchromatic film became the standard stock used by the large production companies; it was less sensitive to light (and therefore forced a change in interior lighting systems), but it allowed for the reproduction of a much wider range of intermediate shades of grey.

Orthochromatic film, however, still had the advantage of being very suitable for the direct application of colour onto the emulsion. Ever since 1896 films had been coloured by hand, frame by frame, by means of tiny brushes. The results were at times extraordinary: the images of, for instance, Georges Méliès's *Le Royaume des fées* (1903) have the sparkling beauty of medieval miniatures. However, it was difficult to ensure that the colour consistently covered a precisely delineated area of the frame, which is why in many early films patches of colour seem to envelop objects as if they were rapidly moving clouds (one can see it, for example, in the manual additions of bright red to the frame reproduced in Plate 39).

In 1906, in order to remedy this problem, Pathé patented a system for the mechanical colouring of the emulsion (Pathécolor), a process known as colouring '*au pochoir*' in French and as 'stencil' in English, which allowed the use of half a dozen different dyes. The areas to be coloured were cut (by hand or by needles connected to pantographs) onto matrix copies which were then placed on the positive copies; each colour was applied to the film through the outlines thus obtained, with brushes or pads soaked in the appropriate colour. It was a long and costly process, which, however, could produce fascinating results (Plate 38.) The use of this system became infrequent after 1915, but there are extraordinary examples of it up to the late 1920s.

A much less expensive system consisted of giving the film a uniform colour for each sequence or shot in order to emphasise the figurative effect or the dramatic impact. The three principal methods were tinting, toning and mordanting.

Tinting was done in three ways: by applying a coloured varnish to the emulsion; later, by immersing the film in an aqueous solution of colouring material (Plates 31 and 40); and towards the end of the silent period by using a coloured filmstock.

In toning, a coloured metallic salt replaces the black-and-white silver image of the emulsion, without colouring the gelatin on the film (Plates 32, 41 and 43).

In mordanting, the photographic emulsion is treated with a nonsoluble silver salt, capable of fixing an organic colouring agent (Plate 35).

A tinted film is coloured in the dark as well as in the light parts of the frame and on the edges of the print (Plate 40). With toning and mordanting, only the areas of the emulsion where the silver has been deposited are coloured. During projection, the remaining areas of the frame appear as white surfaces; the perforated edges of the film are also not coloured (Plate 41). Tinting, toning, mordanting and mechanical colouring could be combined, thus multiplying the creative possibilities of these techniques (Plates 33, 34, 36 and 42). A unique and visually striking variation on tinting is provided by the Handschiegl process (also known as the Wyckoff-DeMille process, 1916–27), an elaborate system derived from lithography (Plate 45).

The first attempts at making colour films by superimposing red, green and blue dyes date back to 1899 (experiments by Frederick Marshall Lee and Edward Raymond Turner). One of the earliest surviving examples of this method is the three-colour system by William Friese-Greene (Plate 46). However, it was not until 1906 that George Albert Smith achieved a commercially viable result with Kinemacolor: a semi-transparent disc divided into two sectors, red and blue-green, was placed in front of the camera lens; the film was then shown with the same coloured filters at the speed of 32 frames per second, and the images thus obtained fused the two primary colours into a single image. Although the colour variations were modest, the effect was undeniable. The invention was immediately imitated, sometimes using frames divided into two sections (the Colcin system, 1913), with three primary colours instead of two (Chronochrome Gaumont, 1913, Plate 48; Agfacolor, 1915), or with lenticular film (Keller-Dorian/Berthon process, 1923).

The first colour-sensitive cinematographic film stock was invented by Eastman Kodak around 1915 and commercially developed a short time later as the brand name Kodachrome (Plate 44). Although it could record only two colours, it was the beginning of a much more radical innovation. During the same period a company founded by Herbert T. Kalmus, W. Burton Westcott and Daniel Frost Comstock started to experiment with a system based on the additive synthesis of two colours. Disappointed with the results, the three changed strategy in 1919, studying the possibility of using the principle of subtractive synthesis, still using two colours. In less than three years, they achieved a colour film, *The Toll of the Sea*, directed by Chester M. Franklin and released late in 1922 by Metro Pictures. The result was achieved by using two negatives and two positive prints with separate colours, cemented to each other in a double layer. Other inventors and other inventions (Brewster Color, 1915; Prizma, 1917; Polychromide, 1918; Kelley Color, 1924) vied for success, but the last four years of the silent cinema saw the gradual but irresistible rise of the system researched by Kalmus and his associates in the infant Technicolor Motion Picture Corporation (see Plates 29 and 47).

Sound

From the outset, silent cinema had an aesthetics and a technology of colour. The same goes for sound. From the start, performers had accompanied the first projections of images with comments and interpretations for the public. This had both an educational and a dramatic purpose: the showing of Edwin S. Porter's *Parsifal* (1904) demanded the presence of actors in the cinema hall, the projection of magic lantern slides alternating with episodes from the film, and the performance of pieces of music drawn from Wagnerian arias. Two actors accompanied the Russian short *Boris Godunov*, produced by the Khanzhonkov company in 1912. For many years, in the long era of silent cinema in Japan,

A group of technicians performing noise effects behind the screen of a movie theatre. Illustration from a Gaumont catalogue of film equipment, United States, ca. 1912. Film Department, George Eastman House, Rochester.

films were accompanied by interpreters known as *benshi* who emphasised the content of the action with movements and prepared or semi-improvised texts.

With words came music. At first, music was improvised on a piano; later it was adapted from the current musical repertory, and finally it was composed on commission and performed by orchestras, choirs and opera singers on great occasions, by chamber music ensembles or pianos again in more modest establishments. Camille Saint-Saëns's score for Calmettes and Le Bargy's *L'Assassinat du Duc de Guise* (Pathé, 1908) is often said to be the earliest landmark of live music for silent films. The event was particularly significant, since an academic composer had finally agreed to write a score for the product of a new art distrusted by intellectuals. There were also many extreme examples of the alliance between music and the moving image: on 5 September 1916 the first official public showing of D. W. Griffith's *Intolerance* was accompanied by a 46-piece orchestra and a 16-voice choir; in the following year, in the Netherlands, Johan Gildermejer made *Gloria Transita*, a film set in the world of opera which required performers to stand beside the screen and sing in time with the characters' lip movements.

Cinema owners who could not afford such luxuries usually had two options. The first was to entrust a pianist, an organist or a small instrumental group with brief scores summarising the tunes thought necessary to accompany each episode in the film; often they were not even true scores, but cue sheets indicating which widely known popular or classical pieces to play (from these cue sheets it is sometimes possible to reconstruct the narrative structure of films preserved in an incomplete form). The other, more drastic solution involved doing without musicians and using mechanical instruments, from pianolas to huge multi-instrument polyphons driven by compressed air, into which rolls of perforated paper were fitted reproducing the music scores. The repertory available from the many companies which produced these rolls was endless; even well-established academic musicians like Paul Hindemith contributed to it. Sometimes 'noise effects' were produced live in order to enhance the realism of the events depicted in the film. To this end, noise machines or noise performers were deployed to simulate the sounds of natural or artificial occurrences. They relied on ingenious and at times bizarre devices.

The fathers of the moving image had demonstrated from the beginning, however, that they had even greater ambitions. As far back as April 1895, Thomas Alva Edison had presented a system for synchronising a cylinder phonograph with his Kinetoscope: while watching the moving images through a peephole viewer, the spectator listened to a sound recording through earphones. According to some sources, the synchronisation between phonograph discs and film was supposed to have started in 1896 with the use of the Berliner Grammophon by the French company Pathé. From then to 1906 many tried to follow the same direction: among them were Gaumont (Plate 19), Pineaud and Joly in France, Goldschmidt and Messter in Germany. All, to some extent, had to contend with the problem of amplifying the feeble sound of the phonograph in large halls.

In 1900, the year of the Universal Exhibition in Paris, Ernst Rühmer in Germany, William D. Duddell in Great Britain and Th. Simon, working independently, perfected a revolutionary idea aiming to reproduce sound photographically on film. This was taken up and developed in 1906 by Eugène-Auguste Lauste, who patented a machine capable of recording images and sounds simultaneously on the same strip of film. However, for some time, production companies went on using synchronised discs. For example, Oskar Messter in Germany (1908), Giovanni Pastrone in Italy (1909) and Léon Gaumont in France (1909–10) distributed short films accompanied by texts and arias from light theatre and opera.

The premonitory signs of the real revolution, and the end of the silent era, emerged around 1918 in Germany, thanks to Vogt, Engel and Massolle. Their equipment for recording sound photographically on a separate film (the Tri-Ergon system) was presented to the public four years later in Berlin. Also working in this field were Kovalendov in the Soviet Union (1920) and Lee de Forest, whose Phonofilm (United States, 1923) involved reading a soundtrack, placed on the same film stock which held the images, by means of a photo-electric cell. In 1926 Warner Bros. presented *Don Juan*, starring John Barrymore. The film was synchronised to several 33⅓ rpm records with a 40cm diameter, played with a stylus which started in the centre of the record and went out to the edge (Vitaphone system). Meanwhile another American company, Fox, was buying the rights to the Tri-Ergon and Phonofilm systems, and applying sound to previously made silent films.

Thus, the year 1926 marks the beginning of the history of sound cinema in the current sense of the term. In 1926, in the Soviet Union, P. G. Tager published the results of his research on a variable-density soundtrack; a few months later, Fox was proud to show Lindbergh, Mussolini and George Bernard Shaw with their own voices (Movietone News, April 1927). For some time films synchronised with records would run parallel to those with a soundtrack; but in less than two years the latter definitely became dominant. Soundtracks were added to works which had recently been finished as silents or to those which belonged to a past that suddenly seemed remote, almost incomprehensible without sound and dialogue (Larry Semon's pre-1920 Vitagraph comedies, for example, were provided with sound for their subsequent commercial exploitation).

Projection

Until the end of the silent era most films went through the wheels of variable-speed projectors, operated by hand or driven by an electric motor. The operator had to adapt the projection speed to the shooting speed, which in turn depended on various factors: the quality of lighting on the scene, the film's sensitivity, the kind of action the camera had to record. In order to ensure that the movements of characters appeared natural, projectionists of the late 19th and early 20th centuries showed films at a speed between 14 and 18 frames per second. If projected at less than 14 frames per second, the flickering of the image would have been too annoying for the eyes and the projector light risked burning the film.

The ideal projection speed could vary even within the same film, either because the shooting conditions varied or in order to obtain the desired comic or dramatic effects. It also happened that projectionists drastically increased the projection speed (sometimes causing protests from the public) in order to add to the number of daily shows, or that they changed it at the suggestion of the musicians who otherwise might not be able to follow a certain action, or to give a scene the desired emotional impact.

The average projection speed increased with the passing years, until it became established – although after many uncertainties and much debate – at 24 frames per second. Higher speeds were used occasionally for experiments with colour films: 32 frames per second for the Kinemacolor system (1906–14), 40 to 70 frames per second for the equipment patented by William Friese-Greene from 1898 (see Plate 46). The opposite tendency was seen, on the other hand, in some amateur film formats whose projection speed decreased to a low of 14 or even 10 frames per second.

The quality of projection was also affected by the lighting equipment adopted. Before electric light became dominant, there were at least four other systems in use. Oxyetheric light was produced by a small cylinder of caustic lime rendered incandescent with a flame produced by a mixture of oxygen and ether. Oxyhydrogen light was based on a similar principle but obtained with a mixture of oxygen and hydrogen. Oxycalcic light also used caustic lime, made incandescent by a jet of oxygen combined with a flame produced by alcohol. Acetylene was tried briefly at the end of the 19th and the very beginning of the 20th century, but was eventually abandoned because the light from the gas was very weak, and the vapours released had an unpleasant smell.

Virtually all 35mm projectors used films whose frames were about 23mm wide and 18mm high. Every metre of film held 54 images (16 frames per foot of film), as in the present film stock of the same format. The aspect ratio of the frame (from 1:1.31 to about 1:1.38) remained practically unchanged until the soundtrack was introduced. No anamorphic frame was devised until 1927, when the Frenchman Henri Chrétien presented his Hypergonar system, used, for instance, in Claude Autant-Lara's short film *Construire un feu* (1925–9). Excepting the films in which the widening of the field of vision was a consequence of changing the aspect ratio of the frame, or because the lenses of the projectors magnified the image size on the screen (as with Magnascope, 1926), the two most important attempts to expand the field of vision are Grimoin-Sanson's Cinéorama (1900), with its ten 70mm projectors arranged through 360° to show an image surrounding the spectators, and the equally short-lived Polyvision system (1927) used in the famous triptych sequence of Abel Gance's *Napoléon*: three adjacent 35mm cameras showing three abutting films simultaneously to form a widescreen image. Finally, we must mention Filoteo Alberini's experiment in Italy (1911) with a machine for a 70mm film whose shooting angle reached 110° (Plate 11).

Production

How many films were produced during the silent era? Nobody knows precisely, and perhaps we shall never know. The few attempts at setting out a general filmography of the period failed because the number of titles was too large and reliable documents too scarce, especially for the first decade of cinema's life. (The problems are considered at greater length in Chapter 3.) According to one very approximate estimate, the copies of silent films at present preserved in the world's most important film archives number no less than 30,000 (including both fiction and non-fiction films). However, this number is probably destined to increase. In any case, if we are to believe the film historians' and archivists' estimate that more than 80 per cent of the world production of silent films has been lost, an ideal list of titles would easily reach more than 150,000 films.

Distribution

When computing those hypothetical figures, one must also consider the number of copies made available by the trade through four procedures:

- the direct sale of films, typical of the first ten years of cinema;
- vertically organised integrated distribution as tried in France by Pathé Omnia between 1907 and 1909, in which the company controlled the film from beginning to end: manufacturing the raw stock, producing the film, distributing it and finally owning the theatres in which the films were shown;
- rental, introduced as a standard practice from 1909 onwards;
- second-hand sales, which derived from the practice of direct sale but survived the period in which the latter was replaced by the practice of renting films.

The evidence on this point is inconclusive, but it is assumed that an average of about a hundred prints were struck for a fiction film produced by a major European company around 1910. The same is true for films produced in Denmark by Nordisk in its heyday, though for an international success like *Den hvide Slavehandel II* (August Blom, 1911) at least 260 copies were struck. On the other hand, various early American films which regularly appeared in company lists sold only one or two copies, or were never actually printed because nobody requested them. On average, a 1914 Keystone comedy was released in a few more than thirty prints, although forty copies were struck of Chaplin's *Dough and Dynamite* and forty-one of *His Trysting Places*. Chaplin himself stated that 135 copies of the first film he made for Essanay, *His New Job* (1915), were already booked at the end of shooting. When Mutual released Chaplin's *The Floorwalker* in May 1916, seventy-five prints were needed for New York City alone. Finally, one must remember that any analysis concerning the dissemination of a film in its country of production and abroad must take into account preliminary research into the geography of contemporary distribution: in 1919 there were more than fifteen thousand cinemas in the United States, and it is certain that any ambitious company had to consider the size of the territory to be conquered.

Before becoming subservient to the United States, the international film industry was dominated by European production (France, Denmark and Italy). The distribution of films produced by the most important European and American companies to the world market was established very fast: before

1910, the chief firms had branches and agencies in almost every continent. Intertitles in different languages were shot separately (as a whole or in single frames, now called flash titles). Sometimes they were written down on paper and sent to the respective countries with the requested copies, or with a negative made for the purpose (shooting a film with two cameras side by side became a common practice within a few years of the invention of film).

If an ending seemed inappropriate to public feeling in a certain country, reels of film containing alternative endings were made available. They were called 'Russian endings' when the print was destined for countries in Eastern Europe, where a tragic conclusion seemed preferable to a happy one. In the first decade of the 20th century the same film was sometimes made available in colour or in black and white, with different prices. Finally, the film underwent a further revision almost everywhere through censorship: copies of the same American film, where they have been preserved, may differ because the censors in each state have made different decisions according to prevailing mores.

Decay

Between the moment when a silent film is shown for the last time in its own historic period – that is to say, in the context of a commercial distribution system – and its entry into an archive or a collection, there usually intervenes an interval of one or more decades. This interval is the 'internal' history of the copy: the history of the places where it was kept, and of the people who, with varying degrees of awareness, preserved it. It is also the history of the changes that took place within the object in the course of time: the history of its progressive self-destruction and, perhaps, of its final disappearance before it could be restored. The study of this process presupposes a fundamental distinction between a 'film' as a generic entity and the 'prints' through which the film is known. For example, in referring to the 1905 'film' *Rescued by Rover* by Cecil M. Hepworth, we gather within a single definition every 'copy' and 'version' of this title.

The cellulose nitrate stock on which almost every film from the silent period was printed is not just flammable, it is also perishable. It cannot be used beyond a limited number of showings, and it seems that its expected life does not go beyond about a hundred years. Film archives are trying to transfer it onto longer-lasting media, but it is an unequal struggle, made even more dramatic by the enormous quantity of material to be duplicated, by the limits of the technology and by the scarcity of economic resources.

'Nitrate won't wait' is a catchphrase in film archives. As soon as it is produced, the film stock begins its decomposition process, even in the best storage conditions (that is, at very low temperatures and in ideal humidity). In the course of this process the film emits various gases, especially nitrogen dioxide, which combined with the water in the gelatin and with air forms nitrous acid and nitric acid. These acids corrode the silver salts in the emulsion, destroying the image and the support that bears its traces, until the film is completely dissolved.

The stages of this gradual dying of a film are sadly familiar, even if the speed of the process varies from case to case. The film shrinks and the distance between perforations decreases, making projection impossible and reprinting problematic. There is a strong, pungent smell, the image tends to disappear and the base takes on a brownish colour. The emulsion then becomes sticky and it is increasingly difficult to unroll the film. Then eruptions of soft dark matter form on the surface of the reels. This continues until the film becomes an indistinct mass covered by a brown crust. In the final phase of decay, the film is reduced to a whitish object or even to powder.

A nitrate film in perfect condition burns at a temperature of 170° Celsius; a decomposing film can also burn at lower temperatures, down to 41°. If substantial quantities of nitrate are stored at high temperatures, the film explodes. There is no way to extinguish the flames: the film gives off the oxygen that feeds the fire even under jets of water, sand or carbonic acid.

In the initial phases of decay, the film can still be saved and transferred to another support, but the cellulose nitrate film must be treated with extreme care. In almost every country the projection of nitrate film is illegal or subject to severe restrictions. In our own interests and in the interest of the object's integrity, we must never try to examine nitrate films unless the correct equipment is available. The temptation to look at what may be in the reel we have just found is undoubtedly strong, but giving in to curiosity risks ruining or destroying an already timeworn object.

A nitrate film can often be recognised by the words 'nitrate film' on the edge of the print. If the writing says 'safety film', we can be *almost* certain that there is no danger, but that does not mean that we are entitled to treat the print carelessly. When in doubt, it is best to leave the film as it is (and we should not throw away the box it comes in, at least not before taking note of what is written on it).

RULE 1

In the event of finding a nitrate film,
do not try to project it!
Contact a competent film archive immediately.
The archive staff will preserve it safely
and, if necessary, duplicate it.

A film on safety stock is not to be considered stable either. The base of non-flammable film produced during the silent era (16mm film, for instance) is cellulose diacetate, which is safer than nitrate but, like all polymers, is subject to decay. This phenomenon also affects films from later times printed on cellulose butyrate, cellulose propionate, and, from 1949, on cellulose triacetate base. The principal traits of this sort of decay are described by technicians in picturesque but effective terms:

– vinegar syndrome, so called because of the strong acidic odour given out by the deteriorating film;
– rancid butter syndrome, produced by the butyric acid which develops in the acetate stock;

– pisces syndrome (or rotten fish syndrome), believed to be the effect of the decay in the photographic gelatin.

In many of these cases the film becomes fragile and tends to curl up. At this stage it should not be unrolled because, if we did so, we would find ourselves holding a handful of semi-transparent shavings.

Decay can be slowed but not stopped, and that is why film archivists are fighting to prolong the life of nitrate film until it becomes possible to duplicate it onto another base. Unfortunately, this is also true for cellulose acetate films, whose long-term survival is connected to the rigorous control of temperature and humidity in the premises where they are kept. Having discarded the hypothesis of duplicating a film onto magnetic tape (which is even more perishable than film, as well as being the source of more complex objections we shall mention in Chapters 4 and 5) or by using digital systems (at least in the currently available forms, which are themselves expensive and short-lived), archivists have hopes that polyester, whose lifespan as well as physical and chemical compatibility with the photographic emulsion are now undergoing laboratory trials, may be a viable alternative.

Reproduction

Because they are rare and extremely fragile, original copies cannot – with few exceptions – be projected. Original copies first must survive if archives are to be able to restore these films, to duplicate them onto more durable and accessible material or to preserve them until such time as the techniques of transferring the endangered images to another base have improved.

The archives which are members of the Fédération Internationale des Archives du Film (FIAF) share the opinion that a restored film should be seen in a form as close as possible to the original. Preservation negatives are made from positive prints and viewing copies are struck from these negatives. For practical and financial reasons, 35mm film is used even when duplicating films made in non-standard formats (16mm film, which was used for some time for duplicating purposes, is now becoming obsolete). Many archives have decided to reproduce colour prints of silent films on black-and-white film stock, unless it is believed that colour plays a fundamental role in the understanding and aesthetic judgment of the work concerned. However misleading it may be on a theoretical level, this criterion can be better understood when we consider that present technology has not yet been able to devise a stock capable of reproducing the transparency and the colours of nitrate film with absolute fidelity. The colours visible on currently available film stock tend to fade and change despite the most sophisticated storage conditions. It is therefore assumed that transferring the original onto a relatively stable material such as black-and-white film has priority over any attempt to reproduce all its characteristics with an exactness that is as ephemeral as it is illusory. Besides, some archive laboratories (such as those in Prague, Brussels or Washington) have developed techniques for copying a tinted and/or toned original onto black-and-white negative stock, then reintroducing the tints and tones when printing a positive copy. This procedure further justifies the avoidance, wherever possible, of using duplicating materials with unstable chromatic characteristics.

A silent film consulted in an appropriate archive is most likely a 35mm or a 16mm copy. It will continue to be so until film archives find a better solution. Some archives provide scholars with reproductions of the most requested films on videotape or laserdisc, since the wear and tear of a 35mm viewing print may force one to re-use the archive negative, at the cost of money better spent on restoring other endangered films. (This is a controversial policy, which we shall examine in more detail in Chapter 4.)

A viewing copy can, however, show the following defects that reflect not the original itself but the way it was handled and then duplicated:

- a double frame line: the image is crossed horizontally by an opaque line, most often next to the upper or lower edge of the frame;
- stretching: this procedure allows a silent film to be shown at 24 frames per second (or faster for television). The method, which almost every major film archive rejects, consists of reprinting some frames twice or more times, at regular intervals. Copies made with this system are recognisable by the dreamlike or irregular pace of moving figures;
- cropped frame: eliminating the peripheral areas of the original frame in order to insert a soundtrack (on the left side of the image on screen) or to adapt the frame ratio to the mask fitted on modern projectors;
- alteration in contrast, due to careless reprinting, or deliberately achieved in order to 'improve' the chiaroscuro effect of the original, or to compensate for the absence of colour in the duplicate or to adapt the contrast range to current taste;
- a soundtrack may have been added long after the copy was initially distributed and commercially exploited as a silent film;
- the editing may have been altered by zealous 'restorers' and archivists (we are not including here the alterations made before the print entered the archive);
- freeze frames may have been added corresponding to shots or intertitles which were damaged or which survived only as fragments, and which therefore are reprinted several times in order to make the content understandable at the time of screening;
- apocryphal intertitles may have been inserted by the archive because the originals are illegible or assumed to be old-fashioned; intertitles derived from primary sources may have been inserted into copies found without intertitles;
- production stills, explanatory titles or other images may have been inserted in the film to plug gaps in the narrative.

This list does not include the absence of colour, already mentioned; a film may also be incomplete because that is how the copy has been found. The viewers must be aware, too, that there is a difference between what they see and what the original audiences saw: this should be kept in mind when evaluating the film. We shall return to this topic in Chapter 4 when we discuss how to examine a copy of a silent film.

2
WHERE ARE THE FILMS?

When does posterity begin?
Penelope Houston, quoted by Richard Roud in *A Passion for Films* (1983)

From the Collector to the Film Archive

Towards the middle of the 1930s, with the birth of the cultural movement that was to give rise to an international association of film archives, the wealth of film history already seemed little more than a confused mass of fragments, ignored by official culture and left to moulder in the warehouses. That this was not a universal rule is thanks to those individuals who – investing time, money, and commitment – laid the foundations of the archive collections which one may consult today.

Their names are known to anyone who has been in contact, even superficially, with the changing galaxy of moving images they created: Henri Langlois in France, Ernest Lindgren in Great Britain, Jacques Ledoux in Belgium, Iris Barry and James Card in the United States, Mario Ferrari and Maria Adriana Prolo in Italy, Einar Lauritzen in Sweden, and many others. All of them pursued their own particular trajectories, with passion and a sense of adventure, with unstinting opposition to institutional indifference, involved in personal conflicts, great projects and burning defeats.

To understand the story of these people, and the reason why general access to film archives is a relatively recent phenomenon, one must try to imagine the circumstances in which they were forced to act. At that time, it was an extremely arduous task to try to persuade most intellectuals that cinema is an aesthetic phenomenon with its own dignity, worthy of being spoken and written about with the same respect given to a play, a painting, an architectural structure or a musical work. This obstacle has been overcome today, in theory at least. In those days, the only way of prevailing over the general indifference was by relying on one's initiative: collect films from everywhere, store them somewhere, ensure, somehow, that they would survive, screen them. If it were not for the sacrifices made by many an unknown Langlois and by anonymous collectors possessed by the nitrate demon, we would have very little to see today.

However, to assume that such people no longer exist would be a mistake. Collectors are a secretive breed. They do not trust publicity and prefer sometimes to die with their possessions rather than abandon them to what they consider to be an impersonal structure, lacking the enthusiasm and the protective instinct which made it possible to save the films. Consequently, all the surviving silent films are not to be found exclusively in the organisational structures called film archives: these are only the relatively better-known sector of a vast, mostly unexplored corpus. A fundamental aspect of archive work is making and maintaining contacts with collectors, in the hope of persuading them one day that bare, aseptic vaults are preferable to the dangerous heat of an improvised projection booth in the domestic living room. It is an exhausting, often fruitless task, which sometimes repays the many failures and endless hours of face-to-face discussions, telephone conversations and letters, though the resulting donation may contain only modest quantities of film. But this contradiction forms the basis of the existence of film archives: those in charge of the archives and their collaborators cannot by themselves search every shuttered cinema and every old house where the last reels of nitrate may lie. Therefore, it is good that this army of explorers exists around them.

There are collectors everywhere, and their number seems to multiply every time one makes contact with a new channel of information such as, for instance, a group of initiates interested only in the films starring Tom Mix, or the Italian comedies featuring Kri Kri. At first, these people tend to adopt an understandably defensive attitude. However, this can degenerate into an obsession when collectors prefer their films to decay under the bed – thus becoming potentially explosive devices – simply because they cannot bear to be physically separated from them.

But those are the rules of the game. One collector in ten may agree, one day, to deposit his or her copies in an archive while maintaining some kind of legal ownership of them (which is another problem, because nobody wants to let anyone else know how they managed to gain possession of the films). One in a hundred may be persuaded to hand over the films, and be content to see them gathered in a collection bearing his or her name, undergoing restoration and finally being returned to the screen and the public.

Therefore, every time one asks what has really survived, the only possible answer is: we cannot establish that with any precision, or we know only in part. Because films are hidden everywhere, as are many of those who look for them and collect them in the most picaresque circumstances, it is impossible to compile a reliable census. One can only say that there are still thousands of them, and that – except for some miracle – they will not withstand the chemical processes of the decay of nitrate for long.

In the mid-1980s an American archivist, Ronald S. Magliozzi, prepared a list of every short fiction of the silent period in the member archives of the Fédération Internationale des Archives du Film. At the time, FIAF had eighty affiliates. Thirty-three film archives were willing or able to take part in the project. Between them they admitted to holding a little over nine thousand titles. These were listed by Magliozzi in his *Treasures from the Film Archives: A Catalog of Short Silent Fiction Films Held by FIAF Archives* (1988), listed in Appendix V among the books to be always kept close at hand.

So, there are nine thousand fiction shorts. But what is a short film?

Magliozzi's answer is flexible: it is a film no longer than 4000 feet or some 1200 metres (if a 35mm copy), running about an hour on the screen. This is a rather generous definition (it is not easy to call a film on four reels 'short', since each reel can be 1000 feet or 300 metres long), but there is no point in splitting hairs when trying to collect information on existing films. Fiction features and all non-fiction films are excluded from the list. The latter are as numerous and as precious as the fiction features, but are generally little in demand, wrongly, by collectors and researchers.

It is even harder to say how many feature-length films there are, but a reasonable (though unofficial) estimate might come close to seven thousand titles. This makes a total of sixteen thousand films. In addition, we must consider the material kept in archives which did not participate in the survey. In 1988, there were about fifty other archival institutions, but since then the number of FIAF members has significantly increased, and will continue to do so. It is true that most of the large archives were represented in the survey, but almost all the other fifty, however small, own collections which are of a respectable size.

Other films have come to light since Magliozzi published his inventory and they probably outnumber the films which have disappeared in the mean-time because of chemical decay. All things considered, it is not an exaggeration to suppose that institutions belonging to FIAF own about thirty thousand films from the silent period. If the passion we have contracted is not ephem-eral, we can relax: a whole lifetime will barely be enough to plough a corner of this field.

In order to know how big the terrain actually is, one must travel. From this point of view, European and North American spectators are in a privi-leged position: in these two geographical areas there are over fifty film archives of international importance, various public and private collections which are relatively accessible to scholars, and a number of annual events devoted in whole or in part to the silent cinema. In other words, seeing films from the first thirty years of the century is much easier in the European Union and the United States than it is in Africa, Asia or South America.

This does not mean, however, that the silent cinema can be found on any street corner. If one is not satisfied – and one shouldn't be – with a videotape or laserdisc of *Nosferatu* or *The Birth of a Nation* bought at some shop, one has to make an effort, and know where and how to look. Those who have studied silent cinema for an article, a dissertation, or to organise a retrospective soon learn that the probability of a great discovery increases proportionately to the wish to discover new archives, new collections, and films that have always been there but which nobody has bothered to watch and identify.

European, United States and Canadian archives hold titles from all over the world in quantities sufficient to satisfy most scholars' basic requirements. Sufficient does not mean optimum: as can logically be expected, archives usually offer researchers a large number of films produced within that country's national boundaries, and send them elsewhere if they wish to explore exotic territories. Therefore one can and must travel. If you are a student, or if you have only the standard summer holidays available, every journey to a large city – Brussels, Washington, Prague – offers the opportunity to visit a film archive.

It is not even necessary to spend all day in the archive. Opening times often force or allow you (according to temperament) to begin relatively late in the morning, and to switch off the viewing table in mid-afternoon. The only problem may be our first contact with a collector who invites us to his or her private archive. Once mutual trust has been established, however, it will not be easy to interrupt the screenings. When they feel like it, collectors have no timetable. They will put you up in their own home, among the film cans, and, if you let them, they will bring you sandwiches and beer as you sit in their armchair, in front of the portable screen.

In order to know what is available for viewing, you cannot rely on the subject catalogue often used in bibliographical research. First, you need to know what is likely to be available (which films are in the area, and in which archives) and to build a relationship with the so-called 'milieu': people, clubs, associations, university departments, cinema magazines. In theory, one can manage without the milieu and look up the two or three written sources that signal the existence and availability of films: Magliozzi's book is one and others are listed in Appendix V. But catalogues and lists rapidly go out of date. Dialogue with the people and institutions who dig into the past of the moving image brings considerable advantages: there is a greater chance of seeing the film immediately; there are more resources for transforming research or simple curiosity into a real intellectual adventure.

The most important of these institutions is the Fédération Internationale des Archives du Film: almost every large film archive belongs to it. Established in Paris in 1938, FIAF was the first formal organisation of disparate and heterogeneous currents which finally coagulated into a structure thanks to the efforts of Iris Barry, John Abbott, Frank Hensel, Henri Langlois and Olwen Vaughan in the name of the following common objectives:

- to co-ordinate the activity of institutions dedicated to searching for and preserving films in each country;
- to encourage the collection and preservation of materials relevant to moving images (in archive jargon, these are usually called 'non-film' collections);
- to encourage the creation of film archives in those countries where there are none;
- to develop co-operation between film archives, ensuring the availability of films and materials related to film for Federation members;
- to promote and facilitate historical research on the moving image.

In its founding year FIAF consisted of four members: the Reichsfilmarchiv in Berlin, the National Film Library in London (now called the National Film and Television Archive), the Cinémathèque Française in Paris and the Film Department of the Museum of Modern Art in New York. Since then, the number of institutions joining the Federation has constantly increased to almost a hundred at the beginning of the 1990s. Beyond the size of individual film archives, and the commitment each one shows to collecting, cataloguing, preserving and restoring film, the Federation's fundamental prerequisite is that its members shall not operate for profit. In this they are in line with the ideas of the great national libraries and of the institutions founded to preserve local and international artistic heritage. From this point of view, FIAF is the equivalent of the United Nations in the field of moving images: it has the same problems where at times very different national realities must reach mutual agreement. But FIAF also has greater power to influence the policy of preservation of the materials stored in its member film archives.

Models of Film Archiving

The Fédération Internationale des Archives du Film has among its members the archives of about forty countries worldwide; their addresses are listed in Appendix II. The greatest number come from the United States (about a dozen film archives in April 1994); France follows with nine FIAF archives, Italy, Germany and the United Kingdom with five. A few nations have three (Spain) or two (Austria, Australia, Brazil, Canada, Colombia, Mexico, the Netherlands, Uruguay). In the remaining member countries there is only one film archive. The other countries, which are currently in the majority, have none.

This outline is necessarily provisional. New film archives apply every year to join FIAF, while others leave it, due to financial difficulties or incompatibility with its aims. We shall deal here with the organisations that are connected to the Federation, because their statutes almost always allow researchers to have access to collections, according to regulations which are under various kinds of public control, but we cannot sufficiently stress that the researcher should also turn to archives that do not belong to FIAF, as well as to private collections and in general to all those who collect films. It is sometimes less easy to approach these institutions and these people, but it is no less gratifying than digging in a public archive, once we accept the idea that those in charge of the collections cannot afford to ignore the commercial aspects of their activity.

Most FIAF film archives own important collections of silent films; some are richer than others, but the value of a collection does not depend exclusively on its dimensions. Rather than setting down a list of the 'most important' film archives, which would be as misleading as it would be arbitrary, it is better to distinguish their objectives and structures, since these two factors govern access to the collections and the type of material which can be consulted in them. According to this approach, the following models of film archive (which are not mutually exclusive) may be identified.

National Film Archives

National film archives are most often state-controlled and set up to preserve the heritage of moving images in the respective countries. Film producers are sometimes required by law to deposit a negative or at least a positive copy of their work in these organisations. This rule is applied with varying degrees of systematisation by institutions such as the Archives du Film in Bois d'Arcy, the Cineteca Nazionale in Rome, the Suomen Elokuva-Arkisto in Helsinki and the Danske Filmmuseum in Copenhagen. The Svenska Filminstitutet/Cinemateket in Stockholm is a good example: it has preserved and restored every surviving Swedish film and regularly receives copies of new films produced in Sweden. The Motion Picture, Broadcasting and Recorded Sound Division of the Library of Congress in Washington, DC, operates on a similar principle, even if the enormous quantity of material produced inside the United States compels it to be selective. The Library's fund of viewing prints may be consulted free of charge by bona fide researchers. From 1895 to 1912, early films were deposited as 'paper prints' which have often been transferred onto standard film stock. Since 1942, a print of each film that is copyrighted must be deposited at the Library of Congress. Prints of silent films are also preserved with the co-operation of the American Film Institute.

The preservation of the national heritage of moving images is also the reason for the existence of the National Film and Television Archive in London, which, from 1935 to the present, has collected more than 175,000 titles from all parts of the world. There is at the moment no law in the United Kingdom requiring the legal deposit of films (as is the case, for instance, with books), but priority is given to collecting works produced in Great Britain.

The National Film and Television Archive is among those FIAF institutions which adhere to a non-restrictive definition of national heritage; this term indicates not only films produced in the archive's country of origin, but also moving images whose historical identity is tied to their commercial and cultural dissemination within that country's boundaries. This does not, however, contradict one of FIAF's fundamental principles, according to which each member of the Federation undertakes to encourage the return of copies to their respective countries of origin.

Great Collections

Great collections are those which, whether founded by a public body, a private organisation or a collector, have over time gained international recognition. Two typical examples are the Film Department at the Museum of Modern Art in New York and the Cinémathèque Royale/Koninklijk Filmarchief in Brussels. The first, founded in 1935 as part of a private organisation, is an indispensable reference point for scholars of film history and, more generally, for those who study the art and history of the medium. The second, set up in 1938, is a public body whose main aim is to preserve films produced in Belgium, but whose importance stems chiefly from the impressive collection of foreign films which started and grew thanks to Jacques Ledoux, a founding father of the international archive movement.

Other archives of this type, particularly well endowed with silent films, are the Narodni Filmovy Archiv in Prague, whose treasure of almost thirty thousand films is an inexhaustible source of discoveries; the Film Department in the International Museum of Photography and Film at George Eastman House in Rochester, New York, which thanks to James Card's drive for collecting and George C. Pratt's researching skills has gathered many filmed and written records on the silent period often impossible to find elsewhere; and the Gosfilmofond in Moscow, whose vaults contain quantities of Russian,

Soviet, European and American silent films distributed in Russia before and after the 1917 Revolution.

Regional Film Archives

Regional film archives arise out of political decentralisation or the growth of autonomous cultural or administrative entities. In some countries, like Italy, these processes have had uneven or contradictory results, leading to the creation of institutes that exist on paper but have little operative or decision-making power. Elsewhere, the same circumstances have had better results, with archives far from the capital helping the state archives to find films and to spread the culture of cinema.

A significant example of this is the Filmoteca de la Generalitat Valenciana, which quickly established itself as one of the most enterprising film institutions in Spain, a country with no less than ten film archives, three of which are FIAF members, the main one being the Filmoteca Española. The State Archives in Perth, established in 1969, are devoted mainly to recovering films produced and shot in Western Australia. Fostering the local heritage of moving images is also the aim of two archives that are not strictly regional, the Scottish Film Archive in Glasgow and the Kinoteka na Makedonija in Skopje.

City Film Archives

These local archives have been born from the same spirit of decentralisation as the regional archives, but they have very varied aims. The Cineteca del Friuli – in whose office in Gemona the Giornate del Cinema Muto in Pordenone are organised – and the Cineteca del Comune di Bologna have come to prominence among Italian archives, which elsewhere are often dangerously stifled by politics and bureaucracy. Other examples are the Cinémathèque de Toulouse, whose instigator was another great theoretician of film archives, Raymond Borde; and the Cinémathèque Municipale de Luxembourg, the embodiment of the dream of a collector, Fred Junck, in a cinephile sanctuary of 'cinema regained'.

Specialised Film Archives

These archives are focused not on the national cinema heritage but on specific subjects. Examples are the Cinémathèque de la Danse in Paris, a part of the Cinémathèque Française; the Musée du Cinéma de Lyon in Villeurbanne, devoted to the Lumière legacy; the National Center for Jewish Film (Waltham, Massachusetts); the Filmoteca Vaticana, where works with a religious theme are preserved; and the Department of Film in the Imperial War Museum, London, where material on the two world wars, produced in Britain, Germany, Russia, Italy and Japan, is collected along with more general material on the military operations of British or Commonwealth forces from 1914 onwards.

'Programming' Film Archives

These archives specialise in the public screening of films collected and restored by the archive staff, or found in other commercial and cultural institutions.

One of the brightest examples within FIAF is the Münchner Stadtmuseum/ Filmmuseum, an archive which in principle is a part of the network of 'local' institutions, but whose prestige is linked – above all because of Enno Patalas, a prophet of the 'preserve, restore, show' philosophy – to the reconstruction and exhibition of films (especially German films) which have not otherwise been made available in their complete form.

An excellent programming policy also distinguishes the Cinémathèque Québecoise in Montreal, the Cinemateca Uruguaya in Montevideo, the Pacific Film Archive in Berkeley, California, and the Cinémathèque Royale de Belgique, the only archive in the world with an auditorium devoted exclusively to the screening of silent films with musical accompaniment.

University Film Archives

Two excellent examples are in the United States: the Wisconsin Center for Film and Theater Research in Madison, and the UCLA Film and Television Archive in Los Angeles. Their aims soon broadened beyond their original academic remit to include the restoration of films, just like the large film archives. Being the result of a fashionable tendency in the 1960s, which differentiated between film archives and film libraries, university film archives pay particular attention to access to the collections. Some are experimenting with methods of consulting the moving images which provide alternatives to the photographic base.

Film Museums

These are museums which not only preserve and show moving images but also display the artefacts associated with cinematography: cameras and projectors; posters, sound items, scripts, publicity materials, ephemera; objects belonging to a time before the invention of the moving photographic image. A spectacular collection of items produced in the period of so-called 'pre-cinema' can be found in the Museo Nazionale del Cinema in Turin; the George Eastman House in Rochester, New York, has an impressive range of cameras and projectors from the first thirty years of cinema, sometimes in prototypes which can no longer be found elsewhere. As well as very rich collections, the Musée Henri Langlois in the Cinémathèque Française and the Musée du Cinéma linked to the Cinémathèque Royale de Belgique devote particular attention to historiographical education. A similar role is played by two other non-FIAF institutions, the Museum of the Moving Image in London and the American Museum of the Moving Image in Astoria, New York.

Finally, apart from the film archives in developing countries (created in order to stop the systematic destruction of moving images from the colonial and postcolonial eras), there are the so-called 'spontaneous' archives and museums which are the result of the drive and initiative of individual specialists. Among those institutions closest to FIAF's methods and aims, we should mention at least the Cinémathèque Méliès in Paris, the Cinema Museum in London and the Barnes Museum of Cinematography in St Ives, Cornwall. A full list would be virtually impossible to compile, and it would also be unjust to those who are not keen to be known or who do not easily open their doors to just anyone. Keen researchers should contact the film archives whose statutes expressly allow public access: the staff there will be able to give students the most useful names and addresses.

The Searchers

As we said earlier, in order to study silent cinema you must be prepared to travel. Little or no research can be completed in this subject – whether by way of articles, books or theses – without the aid of the archives that hold the largest selections of period films and possess the equipment needed to consult them. That these archives may be a long way away is no reason to ignore them and should not deter us. The evolution of the international film archive movement is so fast that almost every film archive in the world is adapting, despite technical and financial difficulties, to the standards of the most prestigious European and American models. Everywhere, from Lisbon to Wellington, from Bangkok to Santiago, there is work enough to last for decades.

Outside Europe and North America, one must first choose the archive which corresponds most closely to the chosen research project. Getting to it will take time and money. If one manages to reach the less-frequented national archives, so much the better: the most remote collections hide treasures which few other people have been fortunate enough to see. However, much depends on what one can obtain from the archives that have little or nothing in common with FIAF: private collections and corporate companies. In the former, we shall find the kind of behaviour already mentioned: secrecy, suspicion, a personalised relation with the researcher, independence from (or hostility towards) film archives whose activity is controlled by public funds. Making contact with the raiders of the lost nitrate is not easy, but a constant attendance at the Giornate del Cinema Muto in Pordenone, Italy, the Cinefest in Syracuse, New York, and countless, though little-publicised, collectors' conventions organised yearly throughout the world (as well as reading two periodicals, *The Big Reel* and *Classic Images*, both published in the United States) usually guarantees a notebook full of useful addresses and information.

There are also commercial companies exploiting the cinema of the past for profit by locating, reprinting and selling specific images. Such organisations may not wish to respond to the needs of the researcher, but nothing is lost by trying. Try, in particular, production and distribution companies. Their archives are at times vast and their addresses can be found in national corporate yearbooks. Try also firms specialising in providing stock footage, local historical societies, and agencies which lend films for educational purposes, where these still exist. In some large corporate firms there is often a historical archive of sorts, and it may be possible to find something useful in their offices. In addition, there are political, military, industrial and trade organisations where films (especially non-fiction) are kept which are often impossible to find elsewhere. Access to what could be one of the most important 'specialised' archives in the world, the Pentagon archives in Washington, DC, is virtually impossible, but elsewhere there are good opportunities for research, especially if one has good credentials and a well defined, realistic project.

Finally, have you ever tried asking your neighbour, relatives in the countryside, former cinema proprietors, the team working on the demolition of your local cinema? Did you know that large collections of silent films were found in an abandoned swimming-pool in the Yukon, in a barn in Illinois, in the flea-markets of a remote French province, and that an extraordinary work, *Kurutta Ippeiji* (*A Page of Madness*, 1926), was found, in 1971, in the garden of the house where the director, Teinosuke Kinugasa, had lived?

3
RESEARCH MATERIAL

Although our information is false, we do not guarantee it.
Erik Satie

Why Do We Need Written Sources?

A study of film history based exclusively on paper documents is almost always bound to remain incomplete unless the subject in question is no more than tangential to the production of moving images, such as distribution, the architecture and design of cinemas, the patent wars, and so on. In any event, even in such cases, it would still be useful to know which films were distributed; what was the relation between the images projected onto the screen and the space that surrounded them; to what model of perception the rival technologies and patented inventions referred. On the other hand, an analysis of silent films that does not take into account the publications available at that time and the in-depth studies derived from them is equally bound to remain inadequate. For research to stand a chance of success, one must have information that only books, articles and magazines can offer. It is true that the skill to identify a film and to recognise a production company's or a period's typical style is acquired only by watching and carefully studying hundreds of films. However, many secrets are buried in the pages of periodicals, catalogues, memoirs and legal notes. Without these documents films are silent witnesses of indecipherable projects and ambitions.

Moreover, whenever we study the past, it is useful to have some basic knowledge of other disciplines such as literature, music, architecture, politics and economics relevant to the period. In addition, a familiarity with legal dimensions helps, as does a knowledge of the history of fashion, of uniforms and railway lines, of colonial wars and of car licence numbers. Having seen thousands of films is no reason to underestimate the importance of a wide-ranging general culture; the rest, the so-called 'specialised literature', is little more than a tool of the trade, like the viewing table and a well organised filing system.

Although they are not always easy to find, the key preliminary texts on early film history are fairly few. A bibliography of about a hundred titles published during the silent era, thoroughly examined, guarantees a sound basis. The number of specialised studies from recent times is vast, but on closer inspection of the roughly five hundred books currently available on the subject, no more than forty or fifty titles are really vital. They are the ones containing the essential information. The others – whilst some may be read simply for pleasure – will be useful mainly or exclusively as a source of inspiration, to find or identify a quotation, for textual details or pointers to other written sources. If one is not a collector – in which case the following advice is useless – vast amounts of bookshelf space are not the first requirement. Library collections, in film archives and public institutions, exist precisely for this purpose. On the other hand, you do need the books that you will have to consult continuously, the ones which wear out through use and which, at some moment or another, are likely to provide precious clues, even though you may have investigated dozens of different subjects via the most disparate research methods.

An attempt is made in Appendix V to provide an outline of a basic bibliography for research into silent cinema. The list of recommended titles has been kept within manageable proportions, so that it will not be necessary to cultivate this interest at the price of abandoning the purchase of other books, listening to music, or subscribing to non-film periodicals. Here I want to concentrate on describing research materials in general: to discover what they are for; to establish what we can draw from them; and, above all, to learn how not to fall into their traps by distinguishing between what they can or cannot tell us.

Primary Sources

With the birth of photography, around 1830, a new form of visual expression announced its existence to the world not only through the objects it produced but also through the written word. This phenomenon had no precedent: it was as if the invention wanted to present and judge itself together with and at the very same time as the rise of the techniques and projects which gave it life. The phenomenon recurred a few decades later, in the early days of moving photography: scientific publications, theatre magazines, intellectuals and the press all pounced on the cinema, explaining how it worked and how it could work better, on what conditions society could admit it without endangering public morality, and why the world of culture should incorporate or reject it.

The amount of documents produced on this subject in a little over thirty years is so massive that collecting them all is a hopeless task. Many have been lost or destroyed, because few people thought them worth preserving. This should not surprise us: civilisation in the late 19th and early 20th centuries was already affected by the frenzy of the ephemeral, throwing away after use artefacts which today we believe to be extremely important: the architecture of the Universal Exhibitions, pulp fiction, the operettas of Meilhac and Halévy. That material, which was mostly considered to be of such low status that even national libraries often disdained to collect it, constitutes the primary source material for studying the silent cinema. In this context, 'primary source' does not simply refer to the films, to the surviving copies, but includes the written material – whether published or not – from the period of the films' distribution. Finding the extant material of this kind is easier today than it was at the time of the great film historians such as Georges Sadoul or Jean Mitry, but what we have is only a tiny part of what we could have had. However, there is no point complaining. Tackling historical research means respecting some rules of the game, and one of the most important is to take into account, with the necessary perspicacity, the fact that existing information is incomplete. In a way, history has already selected what we shall or shall not be able to know, leaving us the possibility and the responsibility of interpreting the gaps on the basis of the surviving fragments.

On the other hand, these fragments are essential. We can do without many secondary sources, and we must be very cautious with most filmographies, on principle, but we cannot claim to know the silent cinema if we cannot find our way among the vast galaxy of surviving papers: production lists, photographs, actors' memoirs, account books, legal documents, telegrams, reviews, posters, music scores, copyrights and minutes of meetings. Some fragments are even more difficult to gain access to: projectors, cameras, costumes, architectural structures, processing equipment. Film museums exist for their preservation too, and these items should be organised, visited and consulted with the same care and attention one would devote to a rare book.

Trade periodicals, which sprang up a few years after the birth of the moving image, are the sources on which all previous historians have drawn, more or less systematically. By leafing through a volume, it is often possible to establish which magazines were examined by a certain author and which were not, but we would do better to spend our time consulting the magazines directly, and as often as possible. In some countries, film archives are well stocked with such magazines, but it is equally important to visit national libraries and, if necessary, to reproduce for everyday use as many pages as possible of articles, lists of film releases and addresses of production companies.

In the English-speaking countries, obligatory destinations are the British Film Institute in London and the Library of Congress in Washington, DC, which own excellent collections of periodicals published in Britain and the United States. But magazines in English are not enough, and they are not the most important sources of information if one is interested in French, German or Italian cinema. There was a time when anyone wishing to consult foreign periodicals had no alternative but to travel to the country in question, just as one must travel in order to see the films. Things have improved now that several titles are on microfilm or have been stored on other media and can be sent by mail, bought and reproduced (this also means that the original, frequently printed on poor quality paper unable to withstand the assault of a platoon of researchers, can be left undisturbed).

If two or three years are to be spent researching French silent cinema, we should certainly consider, for example, buying the relevant volumes of French magazines on microfilm and consulting them in the nearest library that has a microfilm reader. This is not a negligible investment, but it is a wise one: it saves trouble; it provides us with an important research tool, and once the research is finished, we can always sell the microfilm for a price close to what we paid for it. If, however, your interest in film history is a longer-term preoccupation, you might even consider buying a portable microfilm reader which you can carry home in a briefcase and use anywhere, on a corner of your desk or on a shelf. It is more expensive, but still less than one would spend on a modest personal computer. For instance, the reasonably priced Vidiolog Lunbex model can be ordered from Lunbex, Box 667, 13122 Nacka, Sweden.

Film magazines of the silent period are so numerous that they require a bibliography of their own, and there is no room here to list them all. The names of some, however, crop up regularly and represent the research territory from which we can draw a crucial part of our knowledge. This does not mean that a familiarity with these magazines exempts us from consulting others, but they will do for a start, and one has to start somewhere.

The bibliographical list in Appendix V contains the titles of the main film periodicals published during the silent period in France, the United States, Italy, Germany, Russia, Denmark and Sweden. In these countries, in different periods and circumstances, film production played a role of international significance. On the other hand, no mention is made in Appendix V of such important magazines as the Japanese *Kinema Record* or the Brazilian *Raio X*. These omissions are not due to some Eurocentric bias on the part of the bibliographer or because knowledge of these publications is deemed superfluous, but because the cinema of the early years expanded as an art and an industry from the above-mentioned countries in Europe and America to the rest of the world. Those who embark on a study of the film histories of Africa, Asia, Australasia and South America can turn to national cinema histories (though they are not plentiful), or they have to undertake ground-breaking research in the appropriate national libraries.

For the time being, it is more important to know how to work with magazines on silent cinema than whether a bibliography is exhaustive or not. Working with old magazines is never as simple as consulting a book neatly divided into chapters and with an index, or even consulting a modern specialised magazine. Leafing through an old periodical is both a pleasure and an adventure for the eyes: it is like travelling in a time machine, and reliving – with no filters of any kind – the enthusiasms and tensions of a project in process. But it is an adventure that requires patience, precision and a certain amount of unrelenting stubbornness.

RULE 2
Every contemporary document on silent cinema
should be consulted analytically
rather than selectively.

In other words, if we consult a silent film magazine to find information about our subject, we should (ideally) consult all of it. It seems madness, but we must resign ourselves to the idea that a piece of essential information could be in a tiny recess of the most insignificant article. American specialists often asked the Italian film historian Davide Turconi where he found the cast and credits of films about which little or nothing is known in the United States. Turconi candidly replied that the columns of answers to readers' questions in American magazines sometimes contain facts which are virtually impossible to find elsewhere, and among them one often finds the names of actors in a film.

If we decide to study the films of Frank Borzage we could be satisfied with the existing filmographies, but a glance at the magazines of the time reveals that the circumstances of his beginnings in cinema are still unclear. Before becoming a director, Borzage acted in several films. Some of the titles are still unknown, as are the names of their scriptwriters, technicians and other actors. So, if we want to do things thoroughly, we should use the published filmographies as provisional reference points, diving headlong into the pages of *The Moving Picture World* and the other magazines of the time when Borzage had his apprenticeship.

Film titles, patents for new types of film stock, projectors or cameras, companies starting up, winding down or changing name, portraits of unknown celebrities, embryonic theories, projects for films which would never be released, meetings between directors, dates of birth and death, complaints and denials, debates on political or educational subjects – we can expect to find none of these items if we are content merely to scan the headlines, skipping the often mediocre and repetitive articles, in small print, where for every useful snippet of information one has to sift through thousands of words quite superfluous to one's aims. It may be that Borzage's silent cinema interests us because of what he did as a director, and it may be that his films alone are the subject of our research. However, we may discover that Borzage made a film which is not in any filmography, and that the film still exists. Why deny this possibility? Of course, finding a lost Borzage is a happy, though rare occurrence, but if we lack the means to determine the authorship of a newly discovered film, that is one golden opportunity lost. As François Truffaut used to say, one must deserve coincidences.

A similar argument is true for other primary sources from which any research on cinema, and not just silent cinema, draws its inspiration and substance:

– books: projection manuals, histories of the cinema written when cinema did not yet have a history, instructions on the treatment of film in the laboratory, first attempts at formulating theories, biographical writings, memoirs, discussions on the morality and amorality of the moving image, stories and novels based on the production and screening of films;
– production materials: contracts, regulations, correspondence between producers, directors, actors, scriptwriters and distributors, scripts, shooting and tinting lists, musical scores, publicity releases, shipment registers, letters to administration offices;
– production stills from which we might be able to identify an actor's face, a set component typical of this or that production company, an interesting piece of lighting equipment;
– film posters, which have an aesthetic value in themselves, produced by

artists who often deserve the same attention that is usually paid to the works they advertised;

– unpublished manuscripts: memos, statements, projects that were never realised, viewing notes, letters, diaries and many other things, down to scrapbooks of newspaper cuttings and postcards with dedications; cinema programmes; glass slides publicising forthcoming films.

Any object connected to the moment when silent cinema entered the lives of spectators from the end of the 19th century to the early 20th century potentially contains historical data.

The preferred sources of filmographers (such as catalogues, production and censorship bulletins) are quite another matter. We shall talk about them shortly. First, it is necessary to mention the contemporary sources which one cannot consult in the library or in the projection room: the film equipment. Few people resort to pieces of film machinery as sources of information: it is harder to obtain access to them, and it is still harder to handle them without some basic technical know-how. Furthermore, many film students are accustomed to the notion that research is an activity done mainly in an area circumscribed by their mind, the computer keyboard, and the library. The idea that it might involve a certain amount of work on the film itself is naturally (though not always) taken for granted, but this fact is often accepted in a rather passive way: there are scholars who pretend they can manage perfectly well without closely examining a film on the viewing table once they have seen it on the big screen. Having to handle the actual film is, for some people, a nuisance they are happy to avoid, even to the point of renouncing any contact with the film altogether in favour of a reproduction in a different medium.

Equipment takes this conflict to its extreme, because it is no longer a matter of seeing a film in the projection room or examining it at close range, but of verifying what has allowed it to exist as a physical and aesthetic object: the camera, the printer, the projector. But getting to know this 'material' aspect is actually decisive, inasmuch as it helps one to understand better why a film had been seen one way rather than another, why it was often shown in segments rather than as a continuous flow of images, and why these images appeared more or less clear or more or less steady according to the equipment used.

You may or may not enjoy getting your hands dirty in order to find out how a three-blade shutter or a 'Maltese cross' works, but it is certain that creating moving images is primarily a mechanical process, and we must understand its rudiments if we do not want our knowledge to be left suspended in an abstract reality, halfway between philosophical speculation and *a priori* judgment. In order better to understand silent cinema, one must – from time to time – mentally leave the theatre crowded with people and musicians and imagine what was happening in the projection booth, especially when the projectionist was busy changing reels.

Secondary Sources
A primary source provides factual information from the period under study; a

secondary source attempts to explain the meaning of this information in relation to other facts. In silent film studies, however, this has sometimes been done in an arbitrary manner, distorting both the primary documents and the research findings. In some cases this distortion has had long-lasting effects: it has been said for forty years that *The Jazz Singer* was the first sound film in the history of cinema, and it may take even longer to erase that misconception from film encyclopaedias, if this ever happens. This is why we distinguish between primary and secondary sources. If someone claims, without convincing proof, that *Das Cabinet des Dr. Caligari* is the first film of German Expressionist cinema, we are left with two options: to accept the claim as correct, because everybody seems to believe it; or to doubt it and not to repeat that assertion when next we write about German Expressionism, at least until primary sources and the films we have seen have driven us to accept the same conclusion.

Film history is full of apodictic statements such as the one on *Caligari*, not because many scholars were incompetent or dishonest, but because the discipline has often had to serve the myth in order to acquire dignity in the eyes of those who, for decades, have denied cinema any right of intellectual citizenship. Thus it has been written that Georges Méliès made 1500 films; that *Cabiria* was the first film where the camera was put on rails for tracking shots; that, again, *Das Cabinet des Dr. Caligari* was the first Expressionist film. None of this is true. But when such statements were published for the first time, there was probably a reason – a cultural and ideological reason, if not an objective one – for disseminating them.

Fortunately, there is continuous and steady progress in cinema studies, and many of these preconceptions have been refuted or reappraised. Similar preconceptions – expressed in subtler and more insidious forms – are to be found in highly respected books and articles. And yet we should not eliminate these works from our intellectual landscape, unless we want to fall victim, in our turn, to the determinist attitude for which we too often reproach our predecessors; on the contrary, we should keep in mind the convictions and the 'truths' they set out, and the role they played before their claims were tested by facts. Nevertheless, precautions are in order if people's errors are not to endanger future research. The safest precaution is doubt.

RULE 3

If a book or an article on silent cinema
contains some controversial data,
and provides no opportunity to check its accuracy,
it is wise to be wary.

In order to prevent an excessively rigid application of this rule, some distinctions have to be made. The first concerns the right to a margin of error for those who have opened the way for us. Film historians writing in the 1940s might have had at their disposal material which later disappeared, but they certainly did not have at their disposal the documentary and operational tools which today are accessible to all. It would have been helpful and would have saved many misunderstandings and much effort if sources had, in some cases, been quoted more carefully. But the kind of cultural struggle which was fought only a decade or two after the twilight of silent cinema was quite different from what it is now, and there was less time then to ensure the kind of objectivity and precision we have a right to expect in a book or an article written today.

The second distinction concerns the results achieved between then and now in the context of historical, aesthetic and theoretical research about cinema and the mentality that derives from it. If we had to distinguish what is really indispensable from what is not in the huge bibliography of silent film, very few books and articles would be saved. The first victims would be works written with a careless attitude to precision and detail, hastily published in order to rescue from shameful oblivion many great personalities of the past. To most people, Lois Weber, Léonce Perret and Robert William Paul were names without faces: exaggeration was the price which had to be paid to restore them to their place in history. It was as if overexposing the negative was the only way to bring out certain details of the photograph, even to the detriment of the chiaroscuro balance.

Some books written and published in the period between 1930 and 1970, especially in France and the United States, are unreliable from the point of view of factual accuracy, yet they are of great importance for those who want a vivid impression of the world in which the people who developed the cinema, and brought it to its silent splendour in a few years, lived and breathed. Besides, some accounts openly based on anecdote and verbal memory contain important and fundamental truths, confirmed only much later, at the end of long and difficult archive research. Just as one must not automatically reject 'impressionist' histories of the cinema, so it is unwise to place unconditional trust in those who deluge us with superfluous details, vast quantities of end-of-chapter notes and complicated explanations yielding disappointing results. An intricate scholarly apparatus sometimes hides a lack of creativity and insight. I shall return to this problem in Chapter 5. But I want to stress here that reading theoretically and analytically complex works should not lead us to adopt a passively deferential attitude towards them. Journalistic reminiscences, studies inspired by an uneducated passion, biographies based on faulty memories can be misleading, but never as misleading as an essay that daunts the reader with useless figures, allusions and neologisms. As E. M. Forster pointed out, at the end of even the most meticulous search among the events and ideas of the past comes the responsibility of 'telling a story' – that is to say, of explaining the meaning and the fecundity of our discoveries so that others may want to listen to the account and go further in analysing their implications. This, too, is a rule which was certainly not invented by the history of cinema, but which is vital for its evolution and fortune among future generations.

The Filmographer's Nightmare
With the issue of filmographies we reach the nucleus of the obsessions and frustrations of those who study and examine the products of silent cinema in

order to evaluate their identity and meaning. We may be able to dispense with many books that seek to reconstruct the history of moving images by means of anecdotal writing and biographical portraits, but we cannot do without knowing who made which films, when this happened, where, and by which production company.

From the point of view of aesthetic judgment, novelty is only one of a film's relevant characteristics. We may, for example, appreciate a silent film that makes creative use of artificial lighting, yet our appreciation has little value if we do not know in which period the film was made. If it is an early film, it is probable that its importance is increased by qualities otherwise unknown at that time; if it is a later film, ours is no longer a discovery, but the confirmation of what silent cinema had already invented and disseminated throughout every major film-producing country. In order to establish or discuss priorities, developments and influences, our knowledge of the essential data concerning each film must be solid and incontrovertible. In brief, we need a filmography.

This need is far from new. However, it has developed in different and sometimes contradictory ways. If one looks carefully, every period of historical writing – and there have already been several in the study of cinema – has had the filmography it deserved: each with its own standards of completeness, its own unresolved questions, its own methods of collecting and presenting data. None is better or worse than the others, because none has survived the tendency which generated it.

The first, in chronological order, is what might be called the 'cultural' filmography, conceived in order to reinforce with summary information the statements of those who embarked on the rediscovery or the re-evaluation of a little-known personality, according to the above-mentioned reforming tendency in film history. These filmographies, which were prepared towards the end of the 1930s (they began to decline only a quarter of a century later), had no claim to scientific accuracy; they often opened with such sentences as: '1910. About forty films, among which . . .'. The films were, at best, listed in alphabetical order: incomplete or incorrect titles, confusion with dates, false attributions were normal. This, however, was less important than stating that the films made by someone in that year were 'about forty', that is to say, 'many', and therefore that the auteur in question had worked hard.

The results achieved by analogical filmographies were less short-lived. These were created by diligently assembling and copying company production lists: praiseworthy work – particularly because these documents were already becoming scarce – but not devoid of uncertainties and errors. The reliability of the filmography was in proportion to the care taken in reproducing the original data, without distortion but also with a minimum of discussion. Starting from this system, at the end of the 1940s, Georges Sadoul produced his filmography of Georges Méliès and was the first to establish a methodology worthy of the name.

A few years later two more models of filmography emerged. The first – credited to Jean Mitry – was the plan for a universal filmography. This soon proved to be a utopian undertaking, but the project at the very least had the merit of finally making clear the scale of the task facing film historians. It was no longer a matter of mentioning 'about forty films, among which . . .', but of compiling dozens of volumes. The second model, which derived from the first, was the 'authorial' filmography, which flourished in French film magazines of the 1960s. These were a wisely revised variation on what had been done via cultural filmographies. The difference lay mainly in an ambition to be scientific, which may, at times, have been stated in peremptory terms, but was no less healthy for that. The problem was that, once the filmography was published, few people dared question it, especially since it was phrased in terms closely resembling a 'take it or leave it' approach. Furthermore, it was difficult to check, even if someone had wanted to, because the sources from which the data were derived were rarely given.

Authorial filmography dominated the field unopposed for almost two decades, barely threatened by a few important exceptions, until the new ideal of the analytical filmography became widespread among those who were fed up with phantom filmographies and endless (and, above all, uncheckable) lists of titles and names which one had to use as if they were definitive filmographies while hoping for the best. The analytical filmography is still the one most often aimed at, at least in intention, but it has already given rise to two collateral phenomena which deserve to be mentioned.

The first is that of not publishing a filmography at all, because one presumes – sometimes with reason – that it is not yet complete. The author of such a filmography has been the victim of all earlier filmographies, and rather than repeat the mistakes of the past he or she prefers to wait for some as yet unpublished source to reveal the mystery of what the available documents have not yet made clear. The same attitude is responsible for the opposite extreme, which consists of publishing everything, even the titles of films that perhaps have never been released or were never completed.

One may say that too much is better than nothing, and so it is; however, some filmographies belonging to this category are so labyrinthine that they almost become substitutes for histories of cinema, no longer divided into chapters but into alphabetical, chronological and subject indexes. Every title is described with such precision and such a wealth of detail that actually seeing the film risks becoming a superfluous exercise. Each item can take up scores of pages, betraying one of the main aims of a filmography: to be a flexible, reliable and lasting tool of consultation and identification. This kind of monster-filmography also has the disadvantage of being usually 'unfinished'. Indeed, its authors are often exhausted before they complete even a small part of it. But there is no sense condemning these filmographers for following a dream which all silent film historians cherish at least once in their lives. Their unfinished design of an information model is actually praiseworthy, because it drives one to explore virgin territories and archives in which few serious researchers have previously set foot. It will always be like this, because there is no such thing as a self-sufficient and ideal filmography. There are, however, many possible filmographies, all of which suit different purposes, and which are not mutually exclusive.

If we are not convinced, we might do well to remember that an 'ultimate' analytical filmography of Charles Chaplin's films has yet to be published.

None of the existing ones is free from more or less serious incompleteness or shortcomings, in part due to their authors, in part to the mistakes of earlier filmographies which are repeated because the newcomer believes that his or her predecessors had access to who knows what mysterious source of information. Therefore, when confronted with any filmography that does not say where the data come from, one must behave as one behaves with all secondary sources, and be wary. Always be wary.

Who then should you trust? Above all, your own sense of intellectual honesty, which is easily confirmed by stating what you want to achieve in the potential filmography, and how you will organise its essential information:

– the film title, with all its variants;
– the country (or countries) where the film was produced;
– the names of the production and distribution companies;
– the names of the technicians and their roles, the actors and actresses and their characters;
– the length (or lengths) of the film;
– a brief (but accurate) plot summary;
– the date.

Which date? Historians have argued about this since the early days of this discipline, and everyone continues to use the system that suits him or her best. Some stick to the production date of the film, which can be days, months or years earlier than its official release. Others give the date when the film was presented for censorship, which could happen before or after the film had been completed, again within days, months or years. Finally, there is the release date, which corresponds to the day or week when a film or a group of films was made available to the exhibitors; this date is usually (though not always) close to that of the first public showing before a paying audience.

There are also intermediate variations: the first date of approval or revision by the censors (when an earlier version of the film was rejected); the date of the beginning or end of shooting; the date of the first public showing when this does not correspond to the release date; and so on. At this point, it is important not to let oneself get trapped by controversy, and to act pragmatically – that is, according to the needs of research.

If we want to study the effect a film had on the style of later works, the reference date should preferably be the release date or the date of the first public screening: that is when a film becomes part of the cultural environment, influencing the expectations and tastes of the audiences. If, however, we are interested in knowing whether an actor or actress worked for a certain production company at a certain time, or if we want to check that a certain director actually did introduce a new technical or stylistic device, it might be better to check the film's production date. Sometimes it is legitimate to give only the year of release, without further detail. However, one should always specify which kind of date one is referring to and always stick to the same convention. Deviations from the chosen option must be stated. This is useful especially for films that came into existence around the end of one year and the beginning of the next: a film that came out on the 10 January 1914 was probably made at the end of 1913 and may have passed through censorship at an intermediate time. By making clear these kind of details (when necessary) we shall be helping ourselves, as scholars or spectators, and those who read or listen to us.

A similar precaution is necessary when mentioning the length of the film, expressed in metres or feet according to the country of origin. Lengths vary for reasons which would deserve an entire chapter to themselves. We should not necessarily trust the length which appears most frequently; if the length is given in reels or acts, we should not attempt to estimate the length of the film from their number. In the United States and many European countries, a reel measured approximately 300 metres (1000 feet), but in Sweden and Germany it could correspond to more than 500 metres, while elsewhere one sometimes called a 'reel' what Americans defined as a 'split reel', that is, a reel of approximately 100–150 metres (400–500 feet).

To these precautions we must add two provisos, which concern us as readers and researchers. The first is to make sure that what we obtain will be an instrument for our use, and not vice versa: a filmography which exhausts in itself our interest in the silent cinema does not deserve to be written. The best filmographies, even if they contain only twenty titles, are those which give a source for each item of information. The list may be a little longer, but it will have the advantage of giving the reader the chance to verify the accuracy of the references and the use made of them. When one is unsure of the reliability of a fact, do not hesitate to insert a question mark in square brackets after the name or the date. A sound filmography is full of question marks; and so it should be, for the history of silent cinema is a work in progress which will certainly not be brought to completion by us.

A good filmography need not contain many such caveats, but each one must be indicated with the greatest care. One day, perhaps, someone will turn to our filmography for the title of an unidentified film (the archivist's dream filmography). As well as a title list our filmography might include indexes which subdivide films by dates, production companies, names, characters and even lengths and locations of the extant prints. Speaking of lengths, if a primary source says how many metres were in colour and how many in black and white, it costs us nothing to take note of this. The smallest facts are sometimes useful.

At this point one begins to understand why catalogues, production company bulletins and some specialised periodicals are so precious. They are not totally free from error, and yet we cannot do without them because they contain the surest available information in the absence of the actual films. Obviously, conclusive data are derived from film prints, but since many are known to have disappeared we can only trust what is closest to films – that is to say, a document from those who produced or distributed it. As well as providing the title and a summary of the plot, catalogues and periodic bulletins will often help us – or make our work more challenging – through illustrations and codes (numbers or words) which are potentially useful for purposes of dating.

So, we have before us everything the silent cinema has left as our inheritance, apart from the surviving copies. Film archives, libraries, universities and private collections from all over the world collect and restore this material; meanwhile, they go on looking for more. We who must work on this material are left with one question. Since it is unlikely that all these papers and pieces of equipment will be easily at hand, one should at least ensure that some tools essential to research are in our own home. But which ones? Is there an ideal list of the indispensable books and magazines?

Clearly, the answer depends on the nature of the research and the kind of passion for silent film which drives us to buy books and periodicals. Whatever the chosen subject, or the depth of our interest, there are, however, certain books which one should read, and which even a broad-minded cinephile should own in order not to restrict his or her competence to contemporary production. One could list dozens of titles, but it would be a subjective selection; it is more profitable, perhaps, to compare the suggestions of some film historians who have agreed to list their 'bedside reading', favourite books which indicate their relation to the silent image, the authors with whom they have grown up and through whom their drive for research might usefully be passed on to others. Their names and the works they mention are in the third section of Appendix V. By means of this list we may be able to guess their intellectual leanings, or to stimulate ours. It is not a bibliography, but rather an invitation to reading.

4

VIEWING PRACTICE

What an unreasonable request! Ten films! ... No, Sir, we are still not equipped for giving access to that kind of stuff... The library would look as if it's affected by some kind of tapeworm.
An employee of the Bibliothèque Nationale, Paris, answering Guillaume Apollinaire, 1910

How to Apply to Film Archives

Once we have identified the object of research, it is time to knock on the doors of the archives where the films that interest us are kept. There is nothing special about this stage: you write letters specifying the nature of the project and you ask about the conditions under which it is possible to see the copies. At this point, the really important decisions have been made already – that is to say, the methodological questions, which the archives are not responsible for solving in your place, have been addressed and you are now in a position to inquire about procedures such as the conditions of access to the viewing material. In return for the facilities and the access you are requesting, the least you can do is to treat the collections respectfully and, if possible, to give practical help if the archivist needs to clear up any doubts about the identity of the films you wish to see or about any other aspect of your request.

RULE 4

Work in a film archive involves an agreement
over the mutual rights and duties
of the researcher and the archivist.
Both must ensure that the moment of consulting the film
will contribute to a better knowledge
of the work and to its material preservation.

Putting it as clearly as possible, we should acknowledge that the archivist is somebody who is paid to increase, protect, improve and make known the property of the film archive. If the archive's rules provide for part of the collection to be open to the public, he or she has a duty to facilitate the viewing of this material and to furnish the most suitable research tools. Some archives are poorer than others, and, therefore, less well equipped with the technical means necessary for the study of film: one or more viewing tables, a projection room, a library, a catalogue open to the public, a collection of photographs, posters, screenplays and other material concerning the production and distribution of films.

The researcher must keep in mind the financial limits of each film archive. However, that does not mean that the archivist is entitled to make life impossible for the well-intentioned visitor. If the archive is a public institution, the people in charge of it accept the duty of performing a specific public service. If the archive is private, and if it states that access is one of the reasons for its existence, it is probable that the archive receives private or public contributions. In that case, viewing a film may cost more, but that is all the more reason why the paying visitor should be treated with respect and co-operation, not as an intruder. If the latter happens, the best answer is to turn to the public or private organisation to which the film archive belongs. Sulking and taking it out on our friends is pointless. On the otherr hand, those who give financial support to an organisation must know what use is being made of their money.

This is not to say that the researcher is an absolute and unquestionable judge; quite the contrary. A researcher's responsibilities are even greater, because it is on the basis of your behaviour and according to the behaviour of the researchers who preceded and will follow you that archives will take a defensive or an open attitude towards the user. The policy of inaccessibility or diffidence which characterised some film archives in the past was due to the cumulative effect of a number of factors. The first was the difficulty or impossibility of ascertaining the legal status of films, often acquired without the rightful owners' knowledge (although most owners lost interest in their films after their commercial exploitation). In many countries the archive's concern was, and often still is, compounded by the fact that there was no copyright law, or, if there was, it was not applied. The second was the desperate struggle to save images which, only thirty or forty years ago, were of no interest to anyone, or were at best simply regarded as the object of a collector's craze; but it is precisely thanks to the thousands of people who contracted this craze that film archives came into existence. The third is the lack of manners of those who, once they have gained access to the films, tend to abuse this privilege. If curators had not reacted to their excesses with a severity which may at times have seemed unpleasant, film archives today would have very little left to show.

When making contact with any archive, it is imperative to be honest, tactful and tenacious. You must gain the trust of the archive staff, and that is not always easy, even when inquiring about some elementary rights such as:

- the right to information about the films owned by the archive, in line with the state of the catalogue (that is to say, its relative completeness and reliability), and the right to know about any technical or legal limitations affecting their availability;
- the right of access to viewing material;
- the right of access to supplementary information relating to objects in the archive's possession (for example, the dates of restoration, whether something came from another archive or belongs to a special collection);

– the right to carry out research, whenever possible, on copies of a quality as close as possible to that of the originals.

For their part, visitors should make it clear that they are fully aware of their duties, and that they intend to respect them. These duties may be summarised under the following eight headings.

Clarity

Requests should be phrased simply and clearly. The ideal is a list of films in alphabetical order by title, with some basic filmographic information: the date, the production company, the director. If we ask to see 'that American film with John Gilbert where the protagonist goes to war and loses a leg', we shall at best receive a polite letter asking for further explanation, but we should not be surprised if we receive no answer at all. Our correspondent may be an authority on silent cinema (and may therefore know that you are referring to *The Big Parade* by King Vidor, 1925), but it is totally unreasonable to expect him or her to remember everything we have not taken the time or trouble to find out for ourselves. This basic fact has an important consequence.

Precision

The archivist is not a researcher in the user's service. Before applying to the archive you must be as sure as possible of what you want. However sophisticated the cataloguing system and however much it may allow quick cross-referencing (rare even in the most prestigious institutions), the archive staff have neither the duty nor the right to take the place of the scholar.

Therefore, you should not assume that a request, for instance, for films from 1906 containing point-of-view shots can be considered precise. Let us assume that the archive's computerised catalogue allows you to search by keywords (which is highly improbable), and let us assume that the cataloguers have been able to remember which of the films from 1906 in the archive's collection might include point-of-view shots. The question then remains: what definition of 'point-of-view' are you talking about? There are many, and it is possible that the cataloguer's opinion is different from the scholar's. Besides, is it right to conduct research on point-of-view shots in early cinema without viewing examples of films in which there are no such shots in narrative patterns which might have justified their use? This is a problem for the researcher, not for the person who makes the material available. Nobody in their right mind would dare ask a librarian to point out all the books deploying first-person narration.

Care

The objects the archive puts at our disposal must be treated in such a way that their integrity is not threatened. Restoring a film is very expensive, and sometimes the copy which is entrusted to us is difficult to replace (for example, the print may have been derived from a negative owned by another archive).

Notice

Requests for films and related materials must take account of the capacities of the archive where you intend to work. Any plan for large-scale viewing (anything over twenty or thirty titles) should be presented with the maximum notice to allow the technicians to find and check the copies before making them available.

Moderation

An 'average' day's work at the viewing table allows you to consult, at a reasonable pace, two full-length films of five or six reels, or about ten shorts of a reel each. This is only a rough guide, because it is certainly possible to spend a week on a five-minute trick film, and to exhaust one's interest in a single sequence of a two-hour fiction film in less than fifteen minutes. When organis-ing a work plan, you need to take into account the time that may be necessary for repeated viewing, for setting up the reel, for putting it back in its container, for stopping the viewing machine to take notes or frame enlargements (if taking photographs is allowed by the rules of the archive), for making sure that a research assistant is available to repair any possible damage to the film, and so on. Asking for many more films than may usefully be consulted in the allotted time involves a useless but expensive workload for the archive staff and encourages a hurried and superficial viewing of the copies.

Respect

If the material you wish to see is subject to legal restrictions concerning access on the part of people not belonging to the archive, it is prudent not to insist that the archivist break any agreement made with the holders of the rights or the collectors who have deposited their copies. Understandably, researchers feel a sense of deep frustration knowing that the films they want are near at hand and that they cannot see them. Fortunately, this does not happen often when you are dealing with silent cinema. If it does happen, you must not take it out on the archivist, who can do nothing about it (we are assuming here that the archivist is behaving honestly, and not using this as a pretext for denying us access to the material).

Rigour

Handling original nitrate copies requires experience and manual dexterity. In general, nitrate films are not available to the researcher for the obvious reason that the copies have to be protected against damage inevitably entailed by usage. Only after several visits, and after you have demonstrated with con-vincing arguments your absolute need to consult the original, will some archives (and only some) accede to your request. If all goes well, you will be given a viewing table, most often with manual controls. It is similar to an editing bench, but has simpler gears which reduce the damage to the film. If the film is in poor condition, the archivist may only allow you to see it on a flatbed rewind bench, which preferably is also manual: the image is no longer projected, but seen against a source of 'cold' light. In this context, it cannot be stressed enough that examining a nitrate copy is a privilege which is gained by showing a flawless rigour in one's research methods and practices.

Feedback

The results of research should be made available to the archive for internal use by the staff. This applies particularly to filmographic information, which cataloguers are always eager to have, and to information about the condition of the copy. If a copy seems of poor quality, or if you know that the original has wonderful colours while the viewing copy is a faded black and white, you might tactfully point this out and ask if anything can be done to have a better one in the future.

If the copy is excellent, and you tell the archivist, he or she will be encouraged to make sure that as many copies in the collection as possible are up the same high quality standard. An archivist knows very well that a properly printed copy contributes to the reputation of the archive which produced it.

The Tools of the Trade

This section is about the equipment used to see films and about both the active use (at the viewing table) and the passive use (in the screening room) of prints. In both cases we might want to ask to handle – or we might be given the opportunity to examine – the film print itself directly, for its images as well as for any other kind of information it may contain. This is particularly relevant for copies printed during the silent era, but it also holds true for any duplicate derived from them. Therefore, we shall not consider films which are reproduced on media other than cinematographic film. A rationale for this decision will be provided later in this chapter and at the end of the book. If you do consult films via other media – out of necessity or choice – you can skip the following pages and go straight to the last section of the chapter. However, before doing so, it might be worth at least having a look at the arguments set out on pages 70–71 of this book.

So here we are: we have the film in front of us and we are about to examine it. If we are allowed to touch and handle the print itself, we have to keep in mind a number of things and have at hand some useful items which any archive worthy of the name should have:

– *Gauze gloves* If the copy has been printed recently, you should wear them to avoid fingerprints on the film stock. If the copy dates from the silent era, the gloves protect your fingers from scratches and dirt resulting from the film's condition (broken perforations, dust, chemical substances emanating from the nitrate). If the gloves are not next to the manual rewinder or the viewing table, always remember to ask for them. Technicians usually have whole boxes of them available.
– *A magnifying glass*
– *A micrometer gauge* This is used for measuring the frame's aspect ratio, the size of the perforations, the dimensions of the frame line and, occasionally, the thickness of the celluloid.
– *A comparative table of lengths and projection speeds* (Appendix I), to be used for calculating running times.
– *One or more tables of edge codes* (Appendices III and IV) for dating copies.

Some archives also have a microscope with a cold light source (to avoid damaging the print). Such a microscope allows you to discover details which are otherwise invisible on the screen and which at times increase our knowledge of the film's identity and state of preservation. It may seem an exaggeration to insist on the need for such an instrument, but you will soon realise, by using it, that a small semi-transparent surface like the frame is actually a vast visual universe. Some equipment has a variable-direction light source which allows you to distinguish the trade marks embossed on the film by producers and distributors (see Plate 18), the traces left by printing machines and other characteristics which are difficult to recognise with standard examination practices.

With the curator's permission, we may want to bring a camera suitable for making frame enlargements. Basically, it is a slightly modified version of a slide duplicator which can be connected to the lens by means of an adjustable fitting (there are several models available, including some reasonably priced ones). Learning to use it does not take long. You need to know the optimum distance between the frame and the light source (a lamp next to the viewing table may be suitable for black-and-white photography; a flash-gun will be required for colour duplication), and the exposure time in relation to the sensitivity of the film you are using. More sophisticated equipment is available for those making frame enlargements frequently. It is expensive, but relatively easy to operate, and satisfactory results can be obtained even when dealing with poor-quality 16mm film. The most advanced portable model is currently produced by Canon.

The Viewing Experience

The fate of a silent film and its fortune with today's audiences are decided at the moment the film passes through the mechanism of a projector. The projector in question is mostly set up for showing recent sound films. The gate behind the lens is different from the one used in the silent era, in which the aspect ratio is generally about 1:1.33 (see p. 17). You will soon notice whether the wrong type of gate is in use because, for example, the heads and feet of the characters will not appear in full on the screen or portions of the intertitles are cropped. In many early films the characters are so far from the camera that the edges of the frame seem to be intact, but with some experience and a sense of proportion it is fairly easy to work out whether the image's dimensions are correct. In any case, an intertitle filled with text will reveal any possible mistake: you will not be able to read it in its entirety, and then someone will have to tell the projectionist that it only takes a few moments to change the gate.

It is less easy, but not really a problem (at least, from a technical point of view), to make sure that the projection speed is suited to the movements of the characters. The standard speed of 24 frames per second is the result of a long evolution which ended just at the twilight of silent film. Previously, speeds could be higher (for certain experiments with colour cinematography) or as low as 14 or even 10 frames per second (for the amateur Oko film, 1913), and sometimes they could vary within the same film.

It may be too much to ask the projectionist to alter speed during a screening (even if some archives and festivals do this on special occasions). It is, however, quite correct to ask that a silent film be shown at a speed other than 24 frames per second when this is necessary. Many modern projectors have built-in speed controls and then it suffices to establish what the appropriate projection speed is and to calibrate the projector accordingly. But even if the projector is not one of these sophisticated models, a variable speed control attached to the motor with diode connectors will fulfil its task quite adequately. It is neither cumbersome nor expensive, and can be connected and detached quite easily. If projection takes place in a commercial auditorium, the owner will not be able to get away with saying that adjustments to the projector require too much time and money.

What cannot be installed at a moment's notice (but is just as necessary) is the three-blade shutter, a device which remedies the so-called 'flickering' of the image projected at a speed lower than 22 frames per second. Anyone who understands a projector and has a little practical know-how will be able to make the modification without too much trouble. The image will now seem to benefit from a more continuous flow of light, instead of appearing intermittent and tiring the eyes, as would be the case with a double-bladed shutter.

Finally, there is music, which was almost always an integral part of the cinema experience in the silent period, and which a number of festivals and some film archives entrust to orchestras, chamber groups, organ players and pianists. At this point the needs of the scholar and those of the general spectator part company. If silent cinema is the object of a study with ambitions of objectivity, it is important to know what kind of music was performed at the time. Extant scores from the period are usually for piano, sometimes for instrumental groups and occasionally for full orchestras. Easier to find are the cue sheets which told the pianist or the conductor which classical or popular pieces had to be performed during each episode of the film.

These were, of course, suggestions. Simple improvisation and variations on tunes in the public domain were the mainstay of musical accompaniment. Some theatre owners even gave up having musicians in the auditorium and replaced them with sometimes exceptionally complex equipment for the mechanical reproduction of sound: gigantic polyphons with an amazing range of sounds, pianolas with multiple rolls, pneumatically driven string and wind instruments. Few of these precious objects are preserved, and only in exceptional cases can you see them working in a projection room; a specimen of extraordinary beauty is in the Nederlands Filmmuseum in Amsterdam.

Some archives have restored silent films by recording a soundtrack onto them (ranging from a specially composed score to the reproduction of phonograph records made at the time of the film's original release or an arrangement of the original music). The aim of this practice was to encourage the commercial distribution of films which otherwise would have been seen by only a very few. The system has some advantages, but it falsifies the nature of a performance based on a clear distinction between an apparatus producing images and a sound source in front of or behind the screen.

This practice lies at the heart of a debate between 'purists', for whom it makes no sense to show films that do not respect the original spirit of the medium, and 'reformers', who are ready to accept compromises so long as the film benefits. Everyone, however, is agreed on one rule. With very few exceptions, justified by specific historical circumstances, the purpose of musical accompaniment should be to complement the film, not vice versa. Peter Konlechner, co-director of the Österreichisches Filmmuseum in Vienna, has repeatedly argued against any live music in the name of the quintessential purity of the silent image. His position goes consciously against historical evidence and is an easy target for charges of critical idealism. Incidentally, he is also wary of colour, remaining faithful to the abstract stylisation of black and white, deliberately ignoring that a silent film is often in black and white because that is the way a silent film in colour happens to have been preserved in the archive. However, his protest can be understood as a straightforward and commendable desire not to overload the film with embellishments under the pretence of making it attractive to the public.

The fact remains that an honest musical accompaniment – neither 'wallpaper' music nor a virtuoso recital – is without doubt less unfaithful to the film than an auditorium plunged in aseptic silence. Especially when a silent screening lasts several hours, nobody will deny that music puts the audience at their ease, whatever reason prompted them to attend. And the student who has the good fortune to hear a pianist who discreetly underlines some dramatic passage or stresses an unusual gag may rest assured that his or her role as careful interpreter or casual witness is not in danger.

In the archive's film study centre, whether we like it or not, the interpreter prevails over the witness. There is no music, no sense of community with the people in the next seats, and usually no big screen: the film is like an ancient painting, or a statue protected from the weather, whose viewing is permitted only under specific conditions. Respecting these conditions guarantees the survival of the object and facilitates the release of some of its secrets.

Most archives have equipment for the individual viewing of films: viewing tables for safety copies, hand-cranked or semi-automatic viewing tables and rewinders for nitrate and, in general, for all films which require particular care. The most common viewing tables come from Germany (Steenbeck and KEM-Elektronik Mechanik GmbH), the United States (RGI), Italy (Prevost, no longer made) and France (CTM). When an employee in the Library of Congress of Washington accompanies the researcher to the viewing room, his or her first question is: 'Do you know how to use the Steenbeck?' But there is no great mystery about its use. Structurally, the Steenbeck viewer resembles any other flatbed viewing table. The instructions we are about to give therefore apply to the Steenbeck as well as to every other machine (whether vertical or horizontal) which operates on similar principles.

First, however, it would be useful to recall a couple of general rules on how films should be treated. Not all archives allow researchers to handle 35mm reels. This is a pity, since physical contact with films is a significant element of research. Where there are no such restrictions, and whatever the format you are working with, there are two things you should never do: take hold of a reel lightly, by the edges only, as if it were a phonographic record; and unwind a film by hand. The first mistake will cost you dear. The middle of the reel will slip down to form a funnel which is impossible to flatten. The second will damage the film in the area most vulnerable to dust and scratches.

In the best organised archives an assistant will show the films, how to handle the containers (the metal ones are sometimes a little hard to open), and how to hold the reel and place it on the viewing table or rewinder. If the assistant is in charge of putting the film on the equipment, the responsibility is his or hers alone: you will only have the bother of waiting while reels are changed. If you are alone, on the other hand, first make sure that the film can actually be seen and has not been damaged since it was last checked. If you are consulting a nitrate copy, and if the print shows one of the stages of decay described on pages 19–20, do not try to unwind the film. Stop everything, return the reel to its container (or, better, don't even touch it) and call the assistant.

As for safety copies, the assistant will show how to thread the film through the mechanisms of the viewing table. It is very simple – especially since it is rarely necessary to put the film through the optic cell or the magnetic head that reads the sound – and the knack is soon acquired. The necessary information can be summed up as follows.

Speed

The viewing table has a control which advances the film at the standard speed of 24 frames per second (in some models the running speed can be modified). The same control usually allows the film to be wound or rewound at higher speeds, but it is better not to use it for this purpose, especially with 35mm copies. The faster the film goes through the gears, the greater the damage it suffers. Winding and rewinding a film is not like using a remote control to rewind a magnetic tape or to move the digital reader on a video disc.

Some researchers think that, in order to 'see' several films, it is all right to run them at great speed to obtain the information needed. This procedure is of doubtful value as a research practice, even when the object of research may perhaps be a single shot from each of the chosen films. A film cannot be scanned like a book; and this applies particularly to a silent film, the analysis of which requires greater caution.

Tension

If you must go backwards and forwards while viewing the reel of film, activate the control gently. Avoid sudden changes of direction: the film suffers and too much tension in one direction or the other can break it.

Breakage

If for any reason the film should break, or if you find it broken, stop the viewer and call an assistant. If no assistant is available, you could splice the two ends of the film with joining tape (there should always be some at hand); otherwise, you can simply put the two ends of the film together, wind the reel on in its direction of travel and insert a piece of paper so that the technician can find the break and put it right.

Rewinding

When you have finished examining a reel, do not rewind it: the technician whose job it is to verify the state of the copy after viewing will deal with that.

It may happen that the reel has not been rewound after an earlier viewing. The image will then appear upside down. Do not try to rewind the film; the technician will do this. Meanwhile, you can look at the next film on your list or sort out your notes.

Reel-holders

35mm and 16mm films are wound around plastic cores or reel-holders of various sizes. It is good practice to make sure that there is a core or reel-holder of the same size on the side of the table where the film collects (the take-up spool): this will simplify the job of checking the copy and avoid the problem of the film not fitting back in its container because the core is too big or the reel-holder is larger than the box.

Adhesive Tape

When starting to watch a film, never use adhesive tape to stick the leader of the film to the core: this risks causing dangerous tension when the film is rewound. Moreover, the glue on the tape can be transferred to the film itself, damaging it and getting dirt on the gears of the viewing table through which the film will go next time. On the other hand, when viewing is over, fasten the end of the film (the 'tail') to the outside of the reel. This will prevent the coils of the film from loosening and will ease the job of checking. In general, remember that a reel should not be rewound too tightly, but neither should it be wound round the core too loosely. Too tight, and the base and emulsion may be scratched; too loose, and dust may penetrate and the film may curl up.

When you have almost reached the end of the reel (that is to say, when you reach its protective leader), stop the viewer. Many reels are in fact still attached to the core by adhesive tape. If this is so, remove the film from the viewer track before the taped end reaches it.

Caution

If experience tells you that the copy you are watching is rare or unique, or if you realise that it is a nitrate film or a safety film in urgent need of restoration, do not be foolish. Stop the viewer immediately and call an assistant. In that way you will also gain the esteem and trust of those responsible for the archive.

Safety

Finally, although it may seem unnecessary to mention it, no smoking, no drinking and no food are allowed near the viewing table. Everyone likes a coffee after three solid hours of work, but – for our own good as well as the good of the film – it is better to sip it at leisure, in a room set aside for this purpose (the better-organised archives always have one not far from the viewing room). If the film is on a nitrate base, smoking in its vicinity would be extremely dangerous – for you, for the film itself and indeed for the whole building.

The Silent Film and the Spectator-Detective

The list of practical advice is now complete and it is time to start exercising the brain, always keeping in mind the clues and pitfalls which may influence the understanding of the film we are about to see and avoiding false trails and hidden traps. One might ask: why isn't it simply a matter of 'trusting' the film itself? Isn't it enough to have struggled to obtain access to the copies, learned how to organise a viewing session, and taken every precaution to get the best out of a film without contributing to its destruction? What's the matter now?

The matter is that we have to choose. We can take the film for what it is, or for what it is said to be, and try to make it 'speak' to our sensibilities. This is our right, after all. But, since we have reached this point, why not do things properly? We should not stand before the film as if we were about to begin an autopsy. However modest its aesthetic value, however massacred by time and manipulated by theatre owners, distributors and zealous archivists, a print in a film archive is more than ever a living object which asks to be examined sympathetically and respectfully as well as with objectivity. If the print being viewed turns out to be a discovery, our efforts will be amply rewarded.

Films from the silent period have a history, and history is filled with traps. The first trap is a very treacherous one: however much a film may seem to be complete, some parts of it may not belong to the 'original' work. They may have been inserted for a later distribution of the film or even borrowed from other titles. The practice of recutting a film, fairly widespread at the end of the silent era, was routine during the first years of this century. Distributors, theatre owners and projectionists used to cut, splice and re-edit films for the most varied reasons: because a reel had been lost or had deteriorated, and had to be replaced; because the dramatic effect of an episode was considered weak, and it was thought necessary to make it conform to what the public expected; a censorship cut may have made the contents of a sequence unintelligible so that it became necessary to rebuild the narrative structure; and so on.

But this is nothing compared with the surgery a film underwent when, some years after it first came out, somebody decided to put it back into circulation (the alterations suffered by Stellan Rye's *Der Student von Prag*, 1913, are notorious in this respect). It may have been felt that the original intertitles were out of date, but the new ones sometimes had nothing to do with those they replaced, either in style, content or graphics. We have already mentioned that at the beginning of the 1930s sound was added to many of Larry Semon's comedies: it is easy to recognise that the music does not belong to the original films, but who can say how many other amendments were made?

Two copies of Irvin V. Willat's *Below the Surface*, produced by Triangle in 1920, are preserved at the Library of Congress in Washington, DC. In one of them, a French narrator reads a heavily ironic commentary on a grim anti-German propaganda story, which is hard to follow unless you have seen the other copy or you know the original story. All the intertitles have been cut from the sonorised version, and someone viewing *Below the Surface* for the first time on that print may mistakenly believe that the film never had intertitles of any kind.

But prints which have survived without intertitles are in this condition for various reasons. For example, because the copies have been taken from original negatives. Instead of intertitles, one can sometimes see, for a fraction of a second, two diagonally crossed lines on the frame, or words written in ink, embossed or scratched on to the negative, which are illegible on the screen. In many instances, this writing refers to the text of the intertitle (which was printed separately and inserted at the marked place), the colour to be used for tinting and/or toning, and the sequence number of the shot. Sometimes the intertitle appears for a brief instant – long enough to realise that it is there, but not to read it. This is known as a flash title, and is common in copies meant for distribution outside the film's country of origin. Production companies often sent their film negatives abroad without intertitles, but accompanied by precise instructions on their number, placing and content. The archive negatives kept by companies in case of any possible further commercial exploitation were often without intertitles as well. Some years after the Russian Revolution of 1917, when the vaults of most large companies came under the direct control of the state (and later of Gosfilmofond, the national film archive of the former Soviet Union), the films produced by Aleksandr Khanzhonkov were confiscated just as they were – that is, as negatives without intertitles. Most copies of films by Khanzhonkov which can be seen today are struck directly from a camera negative, and if the positive prints have intertitles it is very likely that they have been reconstructed at a later date on the basis of scripts or other contemporary material.

Telling the difference between original intertitles, those remade at a later date and those reconstructed in the archives requires a careful eye for graphics and style, and a thorough knowledge of 'original' prints. For some years, certain archives were in the habit of remaking all intertitles as a matter of course, under the illusion that they were making them more legible. This procedure has fortunately fallen into disuse, and today it is applied only when the original intertitle is in such a bad state that reprinting is impossible. Even in these cases, however, the archives sometimes try to reproduce the intertitles by using the same typeface as the original or printing a surviving legible frame several times until the intertitle reaches the required length. The difference is noticeable because the text will not show the slight scratches and printing defects which characterise a complete intertitle, but will appear instead as a 'frozen' image (hence the term 'freeze frame').

Given these practices, two challenging issues recur: is the print complete, and is the film close to its 'original' condition? The first question can be answered satisfactorily, although not definitively. To the second, however, we can only say that we shall never know, especially if the print in question is unique. The margin of doubt is very wide on films made from the end of this century's second decade onwards; there is no definite answer for films printed before then, even if all contemporary documents agree on a film's length, and a list of shots and a tinting and toning record is available. We might find three copies of a film which are apparently identical, but such an eventuality is in fact so rare that archivists do not even consider it, especially with nitrate prints.

Between the time when an employee of a production company noted down the order of the shots and the time when the audience saw them on the screen, anything could (and did) happen. Directors and producers had second thoughts. Something did not suit the censor, who demanded changes. Distributors received a negative produced abroad and did not bother – because they were in a hurry or short of money – to follow the instructions for colouring the film at the printing stage. The laboratory ran out of a certain dye and had to print some parts of a scene in which interior shots (in ochre yellow) alternate with night-time exteriors (in cobalt blue) with the only dye left, ochre yellow. The next day supplies of cobalt blue arrived, and the prints produced from then on had the exterior and interior colours in the right place (among the smaller companies, the idea of stopping work while waiting for deliveries was not even considered).

From the screening event, when the projectionist could cut a section of film containing an awkward pause in the action, we have thus gone back to the moment of printing; and the closer we get to the origin of the copy, the more the idea of an 'original' print loses its meaning. It is a mistake to believe that a film is an abstract, immutable entity and that, once we have seen one copy, we have seen them all. This illusion, which is common even among experts, stems from misunderstanding and ignorance. The misunderstanding lies in believing that film is an art of reproduction, that there is an identity between the matrix and the duplicate. The ignorance derives from a refusal to acknowledge that the history of the production of moving images and its wider cultural effect is inextricably bound up with the history of the individuals who have been the direct cause of everything which constituted the 'internal' history of the print.

Each print has its own history, and one must unravel it to understand that the alterations which a film has undergone are not just the result of random circumstances, but of projects, conditionings and catastrophes which involved, as well as the object itself, the people who conceived, made and saw it. But you should be aware that the analysis of a film's 'internal' history (misleadingly defined by some as its 'philology') can appear to be a pointless exercise in splitting hairs which those who regard the cinema as an instrument serving their ideas, rather than the other way round, may greet with a dismissive shrug. However, behind the discrepancy between the different prints of a film there are multiple projects, pertaining to different cultures and professions. These shaped the film in the course of time, turning it into the object before us. Moreover, the life of that object does not end with the process of preserving the film or with its showing in an archive: restoration, too, is the expression of a project, a declaration of intent, a relationship between the film and the people who 'saved' it or thought they did. A film is never completely finished: around it there is always 'work in progress'.

Splices
Those who worked on the prints of silent films have almost always left traces of their passing, which can be interpreted. An 'original' nitrate copy usually shows several splices, made for at least three different reasons: the film broke and it had to be mended; the contents of the film were altered; the finished

product could not be obtained without separating and joining different parts of the film.

The first reason is self-explanatory. Every handling of a print involves the risk of breaking it. That risk was particularly high at the beginning of the century, when film technology was still in its infancy, but even today films continue to be scratched, broken, deformed by those machines which Vincent Pinel, former curator of the Cinémathèque Française, called, in a rough but effective phrase, 'film manglers' – that is to say, film projectors. It is also obvious that, if someone does not like a film, or if part of it causes aesthetic, political, economic or moral difficulties, the simplest way of modifying its contents is to tamper with the shot continuity by suppressing, interpolating or adding bits of film.

The practice of editing for creative purposes is less obvious. In the period of the so-called 'early cinema' the idea of splicing together different shots in order to obtain a sequence with its own meaning was a real revolution which met with perplexity and resistance before becoming common practice. Until the time when cutting techniques became an art in themselves, complete with rules and tools for the job, the pioneers of cinema resorted to the most bizarre methods for making splices. All sorts of things were used, from sewing thread to metal staples (see Plate 21). Very soon, however, people learned that the most practical way of joining two ends of a film was to glue together the ends of each section.

Thus, even when it became easy to get several metres of continuous positive film (which did not happen immediately, since the processing machinery at the beginning of the century had only a limited capacity), splices fulfilled two other fundamental functions. These were not directly linked to the principle of editing in the current meaning of the term, but were somehow related to it. The first was typical of the 'artificially arranged scenes' of Georges Méliès, dominated by sudden substitutions of objects and people and by extraordinarily complex visions of fantasy. In his memoirs, Méliès writes that he discovered the secret of these special effects in Paris, on the Place de l'Opéra, when his camera malfunctioned while a carriage was in front of the lens. When the machine started cranking again, a hearse had replaced the carriage on screen: this 'transformation' looked like an amazing optical effect.

The anecdote may or may not correspond to the truth, but Méliès cannot have taken very long to learn that the trick of 'stop camera and substitution' could not be produced successfully by simply interrupting the shooting in order to change the position of characters and objects: at least one overexposed frame, corresponding to the pause, would have appeared on the film, to the detriment of the effect. Instead, it was better to develop the film and join the two pieces of negative exactly at the desired point (during the first decade of the cinema's existence, the same effect was sometimes obtained by repeating the same join on all positive prints).

As well as being the result – particularly in non-fiction film – of the need to reduce or concentrate the duration of a natural event or a human action at the moment of projection, the presence of splices is also associated with the colouring of the film stock by tinting, toning or mordanting. The film segments were divided according to the colour that had to be applied to them: all shots to be treated with red were immersed in a tank containing liquid mixed with red dye, all shots meant to be blue were put in another, and so on. Innovative film-makers could use ingenious systems to create effects of changing colour within the same shot, but this could not be done on an industrial basis; and the rule was that a team of women worked with scissors and glue, following precise instructions, placing every shot in the right place. A curious German short from around 1925, *Wenn die Filmkleberin gebummelt hat ...*, describes the distractions of a cutting worker and the consequences of her daydreaming (upside-down intertitles, pieces of film that have nothing to do with the story, disrupted time sequences).

For us who were not present at that time and still want to know whether a peculiar editing strategy is due to experimental daring, to a projectionist's carelessness in 1918 or to the cavalier attitude of a restorer in 1954, there is nothing for it but to examine these joins directly, and to try to interpret them. How? First, by looking at their shape. If all the joins of a 1907 nitrate print have a rectangular profile, except for one which has a trapezoid profile, and if things do not tally precisely at that point (the montage seems too adventurous for the time, or the story becomes confused), then you can bet that the fault does not lie with whoever assembled the copy in 1907, but with someone else at a more recent date.

It is fairly easy to check the difference on the modern 35mm viewing prints as well: the profile of a splice on the negative always appears as a thin light line, along the upper or lower edge of the frame (see Plate 24); a splice made on the positive copy of an earlier 'generation' will show up as a dark line (Plate 23). The difference is unmistakable, even when the print is a third- or fourth-generation duplicate – that is to say, if other negatives have been printed in order to reach the copy being worked on. Of course, this is not the solution to all the problems related to the study of editing practice in early cinema, but it is definitely something.

Other Clues

Apart from splices, a nitrate copy always has something to tell us if the film is carefully examined.

– The thickness and shape of the frame line (the space between one frame and the next) are very variable and are sometimes characteristic of a specific production company. It may be that the frame line is the only useful element for a first provisional identification of a film.

– The shape of the frame may also be characteristic of a particular production company.

– The inscriptions along the edges of the print, between the perforations, were used by some companies to fight the illegal duplication of their films. Names or initials were printed in characters and wordings that could change according to the time of production (see Plates 38–9 and 41–2 and Appendix III). The same technique was used by manufacturers of raw film stock, who resorted to codes identifying the year when the print had been made available (Plates 22 and 40 and Appendix IV).

– The dark area, marking the distance between the profile of the negative aperture and the shape of the positive aperture, which is clearly visible in Plate 40, especially on the left edge, provides another indication of the prints's origin.

– When the 'shadow' of the perforations (belonging to the negative or to the positive copies from an earlier generation) are visible on the edges of the frame, next to the perforations of the copy, one may be able to establish whether a print has been derived directly from the camera negative or whether it is the result of one or more 'transfers'.

– The number, width and shape of the perforations, as described in Chapter 1, are also characteristic.

We must add to these elements the thickness of the film itself, although variations between one manufacturing company and another are negligible after 1915. It is worth pointing out that details like the frame line and the inscription between the perforations must be examined on prints made at the time of their release. Commercial duplicates reproduce – in whole or, unfortunately, only in part – merely the frame, not what is around it. Other details, such as the shape of the negative's perforations, are sometimes visible on copies from a later generation, but it is very difficult, if not impossible, to decipher them. If the copy available is a smaller format than 35mm it is better to give up, because none of the characteristics we have just described can be examined closely enough.

One last recommendation:

RULE 5

Clues which can help to identify a film,
whether inside or outside the frame,
are indications which should be used comparatively,
and are not conclusive proof of the print's identity.

For example, the presence of the edge mark used by the Pathé company in 1907 is no guarantee that the film was shot around 1907. All we know is that the copy was not printed in 1906 or earlier. There is a good probability that the film was actually made in 1907, but for the moment it is far from being proved beyond reasonable doubt. In other words, the material information derived from the print is useful above all for ruling out other possibilities, but not for indicating the identity of a film with absolute certainty. The greater the variety of clues confirming a hypothesis, the smaller the number of alternative hypotheses. An inference appears to be all the more plausible the more different tracks, when checked against each other, lead to the same solution.

We shall repeat this rule to ourselves until we are sick of it, remembering it for the thousandth time when we confront a short film preserved at the George Eastman House in Rochester, in which there are shots from Charlie Chaplin's *The Face on the Bar Room Floor*, *Caught in a Cabaret*, *Gentlemen of Nerve* and *Recreation* (all produced by Keystone in 1914) in a nitrate copy which appears to be consistent; or when we find ourselves struggling with a film on the *Passion of Christ* in which, during the Crucifixion sequence, Jesus reaches the top of a Golgotha from the 1902 Pathé edition, is nailed to a cross from the 1913 edition, and dies in front of a backdrop from the 1906 edition – the whole in a single sequence (with two splices). This fascinating puzzle is not imaginary: something very similar to it is to be found, in a colour viewing print, at the Museum of Modern Art in New York.

These are extreme cases; but extreme cases thrive in film archives, and we shall never exhaust them all in our lifetime. If we wish to go looking for trouble, all we need do is ask to consult an anthology of early films. Archives have substantial quantities of them, surviving from the times when curators used to put together on a single reel everything that seemed old and which they were unable to identify after the corresponding nitrate prints had been lost (or had been deliberately destroyed since they were believed to be chemically unstable, and therefore dangerous). Have fun!

Viewing Notes

At this point, all that remains is to write down in a concise but complete form the information derived from the examination of the copy. It is important to keep a sense of proportion in these matters: the amount of work involved should be geared to our needs and to the results we wish to achieve. Such a requirement applies, of course, to any kind of intellectual work and the methods are not very different from those of other disciplines. The object we are dealing with is such, however, that a careful organisation of the data is essential, especially when it is a matter of assembling notes about films lasting only a few minutes or even a handful of seconds. Although decades of impressionist criticism may have yielded many benefits, they also caused the film scholar to overlook the habit of respecting some elementary rules of interpretation based on fact rather than memory – perhaps because taking notes is considered rather pedestrian for those who cultivate the keen insight that arises from of the very act of looking, or perhaps out of sheer laziness.

The activity of one of the founding fathers of film history, Jean Mitry, is a paradoxically brilliant result of the former attitude. Helped by a phenomenal memory and a remarkable visual sensitivity, Mitry used to amaze his listeners by remembering in detail shots he had allegedly seen fifty years before in a film and which were now apparently missing from the copy that had just been viewed. Often, it was no longer possible to check his claims, but their peremptoriness and precision – together with the occasional checks which could still be made – had the power to sway even the greatest doubters. On this matter, what we have said about 'cultural' filmographies holds true: when the fertility of the interpretation clashes with the data's reliability, interpretation takes over. Blaming Mitry for having misremembered the development of a sequence or the text of an intertitle, at a time when historiography and militant criticism were the only way of legitimising film as an art, would be like blaming Vasari for not having used infra-red rays to analyse Michelangelo's second thoughts and corrections in the Sistine Chapel.

Today, however, the means for analysing second thoughts and corrections do exist, and it would be foolish not to use them. Some scholars, accustomed to following in Mitry's footsteps (though with little of his brilliance), are hardly inclined to stringent reasoning and may try to persuade us that taking notes and cataloguing them is a waste of time, maintaining that hundreds of file cards and long days spent describing in detail scraps of nameless films are no use for understanding the inner meaning of a narrative pattern or a technical innovation. They will compare this kind of empirical caution to the barren meticulousness of the encyclopaedist who pays more attention to the names of things than to their intrinsic value.

The only reply to these criticisms is to prove they are meaningless, by showing that names and things do not count for what they are but for what they stand for. Some film historians may wrangle over the spelling of a director's name, and stop, satisfied, once the precise spelling has been established. Anyone might be annoyed at reading 'Seastrom' in the first chapters of a book on Victor Sjöström, who worked in Sweden from the early 1910s and later emigrated to the United States, where Hollywood immediately adapted his name to its own commercial requirements and to the simplifying power of the English language. It is, however, one thing to ensure that Georges Méliès is written with the accents in the right place, and another to believe that inquiry into a film is over the moment one discovers the name of the person who turned the crank. Knowing that a film by Méliès was made with a prototype derived from Robert W. Paul's Animatograph, rather than with the Cinématographe Lumière, is useful not for its anecdotal interest, but because it is important to relate the formal and technical characteristics of a film to the equipment which was used to produce it and which contributed to its commercial success.

The viewing notes, therefore, are equivalent neither to a dictionary entry nor to an untouchable formula. They are a working tool subject to constant revision and updating. Their value is never absolute, but it will last all the longer the more we endeavour to add to them information compatible with the working hypothesis we have adopted for our research (even if it is true that its formulation can in turn be influenced by the process of collecting data). Nothing prevents us, however, from noting details we believe to be of potential interest or useful for jogging our memory. We may be studying lighting methods in interior scenes in the Italian cinema of 1910–20. Our notes, therefore, will have to include information on the use of low-key light, but why not also add a few words on the fact that Francesca Bertini was in the film and that her acting seems to be more restrained than usual? Obviously, we cannot know whether in future that detail will be useful or not, but it is worth remembering that no technical characteristic is an end in itself, and that there is a relationship between the positioning of light sources, the movements of the actress within the scene and her performing style.

The precise method of recording notes – file cards, notebooks or a computer – is a matter of choice. What really matters is that the system should be followed methodically. It should allow corrections to be made easily and rapid cross-checks to be carried out. The content of the notes depends, of course, on the research and the ideas and methods to be employed, and that is up to us.

However, some basic information is important for everyone. Before listing this information, and the order in which it might appear on the viewing notes, it is necessary to state once and for all a rule to be followed not only on file cards but every time one happens to name a film or use a piece of information:

RULE 6

One should always distinguish
information revealed by the print
from data obtained by consulting primary written sources
and secondary sources.

The first line of the ideal note is reserved for the film's official title, which is often not on the copy, but which in any case is the first filmographic reference point. On the second line write the title as it appears on the copy if it is different from the former (for example, a foreign release title). Whatever your preferred system of notation – asterisks, numbers or letters – you must ensure that every indirect piece of information is accompanied by a bibliographical reference. If you suspect that the title on the print was added at a later date, take note of it and perhaps find the date this occurred. Of course it is a great deal of trouble, but this is the only way to avoid what happened to many scholars forced to use incomplete, distorted or even wrong information because they had no choice but to trust those who went before them.

In general, archives include the titles assigned to unidentified films in round or square brackets. It is not necessary to follow this system to its extremes, but it is sensible to distinguish those films which as yet do not have a title from those whose identity is suspect or uncertain. [*SOME ARGU-MENT*] is the archival title of a print in the National Film and Television Archive in London, and about which only the content is known: two passers-by start to quarrel because of an article in the newspaper. The fact that such a title is in English does not necessarily mean that the film was produced in Great Britain or the United States, but only that it is preserved in an archive where English is the official language. (*BOTSCHAFT DES PFEILES*) is the probable German title appearing on a print of a Danish film produced around 1906. The film has not yet been definitely identified, although a German trade periodical of that year mentions a film with this title – whose plot corresponds to the content of the archive print among the new Danish releases of the week. On another part of the file card write in parentheses '(Denmark)', to provide a firm starting point for research. Somewhere else note the name of the magazine, its issue number and page, or the archive that has catalogued the film with these brief details. The same applies to the date, which can be entered in the right-hand corner of the file card – in round brackets if you doubt the archive information, in square brackets if the date is simply a hypothesis of your own. Next to the date, for convenience, you could mention whether the film is a comedy, a drama, or a trick subject, though this does not commit you to providing definitions which, especially with early cinema, may be misleading. A title defined as 'trick film' in a turn-of-the-century catalogue can also be a comedy, perhaps a slightly salacious one, and can therefore belong to three different categories: the distinction between genres could change from year to year, at least in the advertising and in the production company catalogues.

Speaking of ambiguities, let us briefly return to the problem of dates (see pages 43–44). Which date is the most valid when we are faced with conflicting documentary evidence? This question triggers endless quarrels. The most common date in filmographies is that of a film's first public showing. However, filmographers often use the term 'release' for the date on which the film was made available to the exhibitors, which is not always the same as the date of the first public showing. Strictly speaking, the fact that a film was released on the 12 January 1911 does not guarantee that spectators would have been able to see it on that same day. Sometimes it is enough to know simply the year of first public showing (or release); difficulties arise when one seeks more precise information. Any official communication about the release of a film is a valuable piece of information; but this may not be found in contemporary newspapers or in the film archive files, in which case we have to rely on the earliest report of the film's public screening or (as far as we can tell) the earliest published review.

Another common practice is to mention the date on which a film was passed by the censors. This usually preceded the release date by a few days or weeks. However, certain titles may have been approved by the censors months or even years before their commercial distribution (in which case the censorship date is useful in determining when a film's production was completed). A film may also have gone through the censorship procedure after it had been seen in public. This was often illegal, of course, but legality does not always regulate events (and more confusion arises). It may also be the case that a censorship board had to examine films released a long time before it was established or that a producer waited a while before making up his or her mind to present the film to the censors or to the judgment of the public. We should also watch out for the unfortunate possibility that a film which went through the board of censors and was announced, complete with date and reviews in the trade periodicals, may never have been released at all. It happens.

In order not to fall victim to a chronological obsession (or to an obsession for any film data), a reasonable question we could ask ourselves is: What is the date for? If we only need it to provide a legitimate reference point in time, it will be enough to specify that we are referring to the year the film passed through censorship or the year of general release (usually the same, except for films examined in December and perhaps released in January the following year). However, if it is important to know whether a film was distributed in January or in December (for example, because a rival company may have plagiarised its contents), then it may be preferable to be more precise. Finally, if we need to know who was the first to use a technical innovation, it might be more important to establish the period when the film was made rather than the date of release or first showing.

As every historian learns to his or her cost sooner or later, exceptions and abnormalities are so numerous that any attempt to rationalise events is bound to encounter serious difficulties – happily, life is more complex than filmographies. But since studying cinema also involves dealing with dates and names, there is no choice. To avoid paralysis, always measure the effort against the result. One can and one must be a perfectionist, but the anticipated result must be worth the effort.

Thank goodness, not every part of the viewing notes raises such ethical problems. And even the film theoretician most hostile to empirical analysis cannot afford to omit from his or her notes the following information:

– the place (archive, town, private collection) where the film comes from, or the circumstances (a festival, a conference, a seminar) in which you saw it;
– the nature of the medium (safety, nitrate, magnetic or digital reproductions);
– the format of the film or the medium carrying the images;
– the presence or absence of colour, and the colouring technique used, if any;
– the presence (if necessary, the number) or absence of titles and intertitles, the language in which they are written and their nature (original release, foreign distribution, reissue, archival reconstruction);
– the type of equipment used for watching the film;
– the date on which the film was seen;
– the number of reels, compared to the overall number in the complete copy;
– the length and screening time, compared to the projection speed;
– the archive number;
– marks, symbols and letters on the intertitles or elsewhere in the copy (names of actors, catalogue numbers, trademarks and producers' marks).

In that order, these collected data on the file card might look like this:

GEH 35 S bw (nt), viewing table, 15 Jan 82, r. 1, 3 of 3, 1640 ft, 18' (24 fps), AK-314.

Although not attractive, this breathtaking sequence of letters and numbers offers a great deal of information, saving effort and possible future mistakes. The film was seen at the George Eastman House in Rochester, New York (GEH), on a 35mm safety (S) copy, in black and white without titles (nt); on a viewing table (we need not specify the type). On 15 January 1982, the day we consulted the copy, the film was incomplete (we saw only the first and third reel of a three-reel film); it was 1640 feet long (the viewing table uses this unit of measurement in that archive), and it ran about 18 minutes when projected at 24 frames per second. The archive number (copied from the box containing the film) was AK-314.

Why is it relevant to know all this? The archive source is an essential document of identity; we must quote it whenever we mention the film (if the film was shown during a festival, ask the organisers which institution lent it). This is something we owe to those who wish to check a statement we have made about the film and establish the source on which such a statement was based. Not quoting it is a negligence one can barely forgive a manic collector. People who proudly claim to have seen a copy of a rare or unknown film without pointing out its source are dishonest towards themselves, because they contradict their own desire to let their discovery be known and appreciated. The childish privilege of not letting others see the object one is talking about is not even justified by the presumed respect towards the private collector who allowed one to examine the copy, unless collectors specifically declare they do not want publicity.

Those who refuse to state where the copy was viewed are dishonest towards others as well, because they do not allow anyone else the chance to confirm of disprove the conclusions they have reached. Leaving aside any malicious intent, stating from which archive a film comes avoids confusion and misunderstanding. Remember that having seen a silent film during a festival, in a film archive or in a collector's home does not necessarily mean that one has seen the film in question in the form which is known to others, or which they may have seen in the past. In writing about our sample film, we shall say, therefore, that the copy belongs to the George Eastman House collection and is 1640 feet long, that the second reel is missing, and so on.

RULE 7
Every print of a film is a unique object,
with its own physical and aesthetic characteristics,
and therefore it cannot be considered identical
to other prints with the same title.

We should bear in mind that the film one studies in an archive sometimes came from a place other than where it was found. For example, the collection of the Swiss abbé Joseph Joye, a huge repertory of world production from the early period, was found in Zurich, then partially duplicated in Italy and finally deposited at the National Film and Television Archive in Berkhamsted. Moreover, the 'internal history' of a copy depends, at least in part, on the country (or countries) where it was originally shown, and the print in question – whose area of commercial use should therefore be stated in the viewing notes – can differ significantly from those of copies seen during the same period in other countries.

The importance of knowing which print of a film one is referring to becomes clearer still, even to the enemies of so-called close analysis, when the format of the film is at issue. Did we see the copy in Super-8, 16mm, 35mm or video? It can make a world of difference. On a tenth-generation copy, *Un Chien andalou* (Salvador Dalí and Luis Buñuel, 1929) is not an avant-garde film: it is an indecipherable ectoplasm which some people have ended by accepting only because the inscrutability of the image can intuitively be associated with the esoteric quality of its contents. However, one has only to watch a beautiful print preserved by the Münchner Filmmuseum to realise how approximate are reproductions of the film taken from poor-quality duplicates.

As a general rule, if you have a choice between a 35mm and a 16mm copy, choose the former. There is no certainty that it will be the better or more complete of the two, but there will certainly be less likelihood of being confronted with the faded moving shadows which, for a long time, collectors and archives handed out as viewing copies. However, if possible and if the research requires it, the ideal is to see every available print: they may have come from different sources and may therefore reveal significant differences.

Noting the physical nature of what you see is also of paramount importance. Unless you intend to study the optical quality of images printed on different film stocks (diacetate, triacetate, polyester), it is enough to differentiate the original nitrate prints from reproductions on safety film. Consulting nitrate copies is the ultimate goal of many research projects on silent cinema, and, because access to a film on nitrate stock is difficult, you must make the most of opportunity when circumstances allow it. A nitrate copy has a transparency and clarity which, despite the most sophisticated duplication techniques, cannot be reproduced on other materials. Moreover, the original makes possible the analysis of aspects of the film which a safety copy distorts or wipes out altogether – colour (tinting, toning, dyeing by hand or mechanical means), perforations, frame line, edge inscriptions.

Is the film in black and white or colour? Notes on how the film was printed (whatever its type) might help considerably in the film's analysis. On the sample file card we have written 'bw' (black and white). Many copies of D. W. Griffith's *The Lonedale Operator* (1911) available for viewing are in black and white, and contain a sequence in which the protagonist, Blanche Sweet, threatens the bandits with something that is clearly not a revolver. How can anyone believe such naivety? Simple: the original prints included shots tinted in blue for the night sequences. In this scene, Blanche Sweet relied on the darkness to make her opponents believe that the implement she was handling like a firearm was indeed a revolver and not a monkey wrench.

This is only one of the best-known instances. But noting if colour is used (and, if so, what kind) will help us avoid gross errors and hasty judgments: you should not forget, for example, that a 1906 Pathé *féerie* can tell the spectator very little if the viewing copy in the archive does not try to reproduce the amazing colours of which the French company was justly proud. Nor should you exclude the possibility of two copies of the same film being coloured using different systems: the Canadian release prints of *The Cossack Whip* (John H. Collins, 1916) are mainly tinted; the version which was distributed two years later in the United Kingdom contains many more toned shots.

For the same reasons, you should specify what equipment was used to consult the film: projection, a viewing table (as in almost every well-equipped film archive), or a hand-cranked rewind bench. You may wish to mention a sequence which includes consecutive panning shots to the right and to the left. If the film was shown on the big screen, perhaps with five more shorts, you should be careful: even an expert can lose concentration for a few seconds and think he or she has seen what a more careful examination would disprove. However, if the file card mentions two consecutive panning shots, and if the film was seen on the viewing table, the margin of error is considerably less. Similarly, a claim that a film has been tinted and toned is immeasurably strengthened if it can be said that the original was slowly and carefully examined on a hand-cranked rewind bench.

Between the note on the film base and the equipment used for viewing is information on the intertitles. In our example we find 'nt', meaning that the print had no intertitles. If there are intertitles and they are written in, for example, French or German, the letters 'F' or 'D' will remind us of this. If the film was produced in a country other than the one in which the copy was distributed, the translation of the intertitles may not have been accurate or the text may have been modified. The number and position of the titles may have been changed, perhaps to suit local circumstances or censorship requirements.

The date of viewing is, among other things, a useful reminder of our competence. Due to inexperience, some titles in our files may contain only scant observations and approximate remarks. In January 1982, for example, we may not yet have learned how to evaluate high-angle shots or rapid alternating cuts. If these are matters which now concern us, we would do well to see the film again (and until then include it only provisionally among our research sources). If the file card dates from last year, however, we may perhaps be more confident that we took note of high-angle shots and alternating cuts, if we found examples of either. Finally, it may be that since we last saw the film the nitrate has started to decay and the archive staff, to save the copy, have had to get rid of one or more shots. If other people notice discrepancies between our description and theirs, the date we wrote down may help us to explain this.

For this reason, among many others, be sure to record the length of the copy in reels, metres or feet (ideally, the note should make a distinction between the total length of the print from that of its elements inserted after its period of commercial release). Saying that a film in two reels is incomplete is not enough: we should specify which reel is missing, and keep that in mind if some aspect of the plot is unclear from the notes taken at the time of viewing. All viewing tables have a counter; some, like those in the Cinémathèque Française or the Library of Congress, are so precise that they allow the film to be measured to one frame and its duration calculated in minutes and seconds at a speed of 24 or 18 frames per second.

The projection room poses different problems. All we can do there is view the film with stopwatch in hand. But this is distracting, impractical and – most important – inaccurate, especially if we do not know what the correct projection speed is and if we are scheduled to see a number of short films on the same day. It is better to approach the projectionist and ask if the cans containing the reels bear any indication of the film's length. Be careful: the label often carries only approximate information, useful as a reference point but not incontestable data. And in an early film the difference of half a metre can mean a lot, both for the narrative structure and for such technical and stylistic aspects as cutting and camera movement.

The last essential indication on our file card refers to the copy's archive number. Making a note of it in the archive is not difficult; in the screening room, on the contrary, all we can do is, once again, make friends with the projectionist and ask him or her to write down the location code and number of the reel being shown. It is extra work, but before considering it useless and finicky it is worth remembering the following cautionary tale. Among the countless treasures of the National Film and Television Archive in London, there is a film probably directed by Phillips Smalley (perhaps in collaboration with Lois Weber, or perhaps by Lois Weber alone) called *Suspense* (1913).

According to a friend, it is an extraordinary film, and on our first trip to London we go to see it. Our friend was right. *Suspense* is an amazing concentration of technical innovation and genuine narrative tension – shots divided into three triangular sectors (with a different action taking place in each), bold positioning of the camera, clear progression of the story. There is, however, a wrong note. About halfway through the film, during a car chase, a man goes and stands in the middle of the road and lights a cigarette. Surely he is going to be run over. But nothing happens. In the following shot the chase continues and the passer-by is across the road safe and sound. If this was intended, it seems that a perfect jewel was ruined by a banal mistake in the editing, or a gap in the script. We go home and talk about the film with people who have seen it, but our accounts do not tally. Somebody says, 'No, the passer-by was run over but the chase went on.' We seek clarification from the Cataloguing Department and the mystery is revealed: the NFTA has three copies of *Suspense*, but only one of them is complete. We saw the most incomplete one and our friend saw a version which was not quite complete. The truth is that one of the cars brakes and is unable to avoid hitting the pedestrian, but he gets only a few scratches and a fright. The driver helps him up, and the race carries on. Clearly, it is not our fault that the copy we saw was not the most complete one but, once we know which one is, when we next want to see it or show it to someone it will be essential to ask for the archive number corresponding to the complete version. Perhaps five years ago the only copy available was the incomplete one, and later a better one was found. When writing about that film, which copy shall we refer to? The only way to avoid confusion is, again, to clarify the identity of the copy in question.

Once you have made a note of the source, the medium and the format, the length, the date and the equipment used for viewing, the presence or absence of colour and intertitles, the archive number and the screening time, you will have only one line of notes in front of you. But a lot of information is concentrated into that single line, and many problems have been raised in this simple attempt at putting together the precise details of the object you have examined. It may seem an onerous job, but the notes are now unassailable. Starting from them, you can launch into the most daring hypothesis knowing that your feet are firmly on the ground. The notes must now be completed by ideas (whatever they may be) through work on the copy. But no one is obliged to accept these ideas unless they can be checked against the detailed information that has been provided.

Ideally, a film should first be seen on a big screen (that is to say, in the conditions closest to those for which it was designed), and then on a viewing table. There is an instructive qualitative difference here. In the first instance, the experience is synthetic, its purpose being an acquisition of the global sense of the work. In the second it is analytical. At the viewing table, the film ceases to be a homogeneous flow of images and becomes instead something we can fragment, concentrate or distort every time we decide to stop at a certain shot, to examine the reels out of order or to study a particular sequence for perhaps a whole afternoon. Such distortion cannot be eliminated, but it can be brought into proportion. If we have no opportunity to see the film on the big screen, we should first watch it on the viewing table without interruption, and then start again. Nevertheless, some details of the film which can be seen (and interpreted) in this way are not necessarily part of the immediate experience of spectators in the auditorium.

However artificial it may be, consulting a film on a viewing table is preferable to watching it on other kinds of media, either magnetic or digital. The eye does not 'see' the electronic image in the way it sees the photographic image; the brain decodes it, memorises it and understands it differently, both in terms of time and space and in a wider psychological sense. A non-photographic duplicate can be a very helpful *aide-mémoire*, after a repeated, thorough analysis of the projected image, but it cannot replace work on the copy itself.

Those who oppose this principle like to point out that alternative formats are practical and economical. They challenge – in the name of a misplaced sense of democracy – the so-called 'purist' attitude of those who demand the use of the photographic medium. (In these people's opinion, the fact that digital or magnetic reproduction is cheap and available to all makes it more useful than material of better quality available only to the few, and subject to wear and tear.) But this argument is more authoritarian than the assumption it is supposed to challenge, since it purports to present for scholarly analysis the distorted and mutilated version of an 'original' whose distinctive qualities cinema studies aspire to evaluate.

For a completely different reason – the understandable effort to reduce the costs of replacing worn-out copies – some institutions tend to support this serious prejudice, taking as an alarming justification the fact that most users are not as committed to analysing the formal qualities of the moving images as their narrative, psychological and socio-cultural implications. Both ethically and didactically, this is an unacceptable standpoint, which risks having a destructive influence on the future development of film studies. It places the film archive on the same level as an imaginary museum which might decide to show the visitor photographic reproductions of its pictures, maintaining that most of the public is interested in what the pictures depict, rather than in their aesthetic value.

While considering 'ideas' about films, it is worth saying a few words on the best ways of gathering these ideas. Everyone knows about taking notes by the light of a pen-torch, one of those which do not disturb the person in the next seat. But when the film lasts only a few minutes, or even a few seconds, everything happens very fast, and note-taking may not be enough. For setting down momentary impressions in the auditorium or at the viewing table, a small portable tape recorder is of undeniable value. Instead of the effort – in the dark, with the film rolling – of finding the right words to describe what one has seen, all one has to do is whisper some words into the microphone; later, the ideas can be developed properly. One should be guided here by practicality and good manners: a mumbled sentence will be difficult to puzzle out when replayed; in order to speak quietly but clearly, careful spectators try to find places a little way from the rest of the audience, far from those who want to see the film in peace.

If it is used unobtrusively (it is never pleasant to be sitting next to someone who is muttering esoteric remarks into a metal box, and even less so if there are several whispering voices polluting the silence in the theatre), a tape recorder can save us from creative paralysis. The brain always runs faster than the pen, and it is sad to stop at the second film because scribbling in the notebook has reached an impossibly frantic pace. However, we must remember two fairly important objections to this method. The first is a technical limitation: if the film is shown with music in the auditorium, we are in trouble, and there is nothing left to do but to go and sit as far as possible from the screen, and to speak louder. If the music is being performed by a large orchestra we may as well give up, and it is better not to take out the tape recorder if the cinema is crowded and our muttering annoys the spectators nearby.

The other problem has consequences which can last long after the moment of projection. Listening to your taped observations in the comfort of your own home is very sensible, but if you do not deal with the tapes as soon as possible you will end up cursing yourself for having used this method. Written notes, even when terse or scrawled, can usually be deciphered. But a tape is a piece of plastic with a limited lifespan, labelled with ambitious yet anodyne titles such as 'Danish films seen in Pordenone 1986' or 'Brighton 1978/Pathé'. Before the tapes pile up – and they do – you must transcribe them immediately. You will not regret it. If you cannot keep pace with the taped notes (a whole afternoon is not enough to transcribe and develop the contents of half an hour of tape accurately), it is better to forget the tape recorder and revert to pencil and paper. You may take fewer notes, but you won't run the risk of being unable to use them when you need them. Even if they have not been reworked or copied out into a more legible form, you can keep them in folders; your only worry will be whether you can read your own handwriting months or years later.

If this issue has been resolved, all that remains to be done is to transcribe the notes carefully and decide how to distribute them among the different files which are useful for any comparative analysis. You may, for instance, have one main file for each film and a set of subject files (for example, films with direct representations of violence, 360° pan shots, films with the German actress Anna Müller-Lincke, copies which have been coloured by a mixture of techniques) on which the titles of the corresponding films have been entered. According to the scope of the project, and to the extent of your interest in the silent cinema, this data archive may include a few dozen or several hundred files.

Frame Enlargements

These general precautions, which are helpful to those who study films of the silent period, hold true for all scholarly disciplines. Frame enlargements, on the other hand, deserve a separate mention. If you have the necessary equipment, and if the archives allow its use, both negatives and photographs must be classified promptly. It is, as always, a question of method. As far as the filing of photographs is concerned, improvisation is out of the question: with ten rolls of negatives which have not been catalogued, memory is not enough. To save your memory for better use, try the following.

1 Note the photos on the viewing file cards, and number the negative film and the pictures taken.
2 Once the negatives have been printed, keep them in numbered envelopes.
3 Make a list of negatives, with the photograph numbers and the titles of the corresponding films.
4 Whenever you make a print, write the negative number on the back.

In that way, you will be able to locate quickly the photographs from the film you are after and it will be easy to go back to the title of an image that has slipped out of your file or that you lent to someone. It is not necessary to print all photographs immediately; in fact, it could be enough to have a contact print of the negative and to stick the small reproductions on each viewing file card.

One last piece of advice. Since you might find more documentation on a film tomorrow or in the distant future, and since the photographs, once printed, should be next to the relevant file, it is best to devote a folder to each title in which you can file clippings, further notes, photocopies of articles, and so on. Even if you are interested in silent cinema as a whole, and not just in some particular aspect of it, there is no need to worry: the set of files obtained in this way will be of a respectable but not a daunting size. And, when data are easily accessible, you will have more time available to elaborate useful ideas, without which all this preliminary organisation is nothing but an empty stretch of meaningless codes, words and images.

1 Lumière, 35mm, 1895–1900. Unidentified film. Paolo Cherchi Usai Collection.

2 Demenÿ, 60mm, 1896 (the inscription 'Avant l'assaut – Le mur', handwritten on the negative, is visible on the leader of the positive print). Film Department, George Eastman House, Rochester.

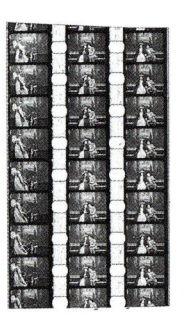

3 Veriscope, 63mm (*The Corbett–Fitzsimmons Fight*, 1897), Film Department, George Eastman House, Rochester.

4 Duplex, 11mm, 1915–27. Unidentified film. Film Department, George Eastman House, Rochester.

5 Edison Home Kinetoscope, 22mm. Unidentified film. Film Department, George Eastman House, Rochester.

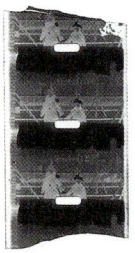

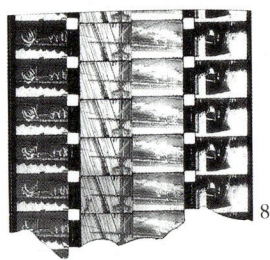

6 Ernemann Kino, 17.5mm, 1903. Unidentified film (negative print). Film Department, George Eastman House, Rochester.

7 Duoscope, 17.5mm, 1912. Unidentified film. Film Department, George Eastman House, Rochester.

8 Kino-Salon, 35mm, Messter 1908–9. Unidentified films. Film Department, George Eastman House, Rochester.

9 American Mutoscope & Biograph, 70mm (*French Acrobatic Dance*, 1903). Paper print for mutoscope equipment. Film Department, George Eastman House, Rochester.

10 American Mutoscope & Biograph, 70mm. Unidentified film [Italy], *c.* 1895–1905. Film Department, George Eastman House, Rochester.

11 Filoteo Alberini, 70mm, 1911. Unidentified film (negative print). Film Department, George Eastman House, Rochester.

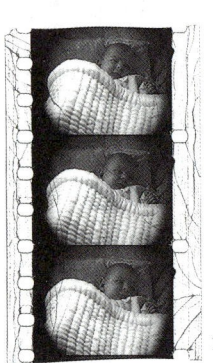  

12 Pathé-Kok, 28mm, 1912 (*Fifty-Fifty*, Allan Dwan, Fine Arts Film Co., 1916), reel 2. Film Department, George Eastman House, Rochester.

13 Cine Kodak, 16mm (shooting test by W. Vaeth on reversal film, May 1920). Film Department, George Eastman House, Rochester.

14 Paper print, 35mm. Unidentified film, *c.* 1912. Film Department, George Eastman House, Rochester.

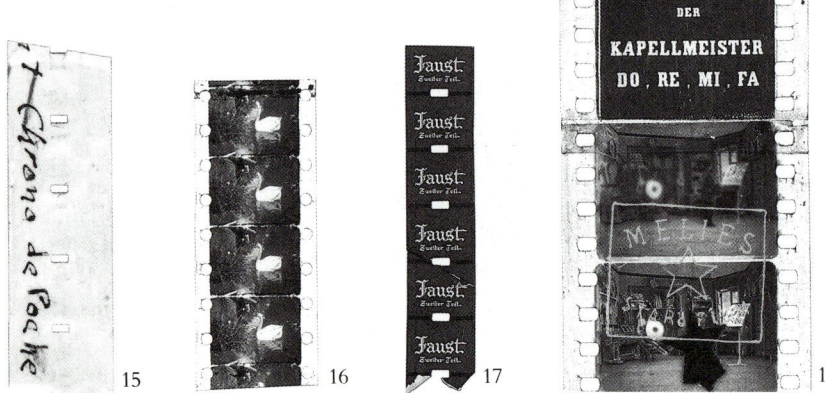

15 Chrono de poche, 15mm, Gaumont, 1900. Unprocessed film stock. Film Department, George Eastman House, Rochester.

16 Movette, 17.5mm, 1917. Unidentified film. Film Department, George Eastman House, Rochester.

17 Pathé-baby or Pathex, 9.5mm, 1922–3 (*Faust*, F. W. Murnau, Ufa, 1926). Film Department, George Eastman House, Rochester.

18 35mm print with rounded-rectangle perforations (*Le maestro Do-mi-sol-do*, Georges Méliès, Star-Film, end 1905–early 1906). The Star-Film brand is embossed on the film base (low-angle-light photography). Davide Turconi Collection, Pavia.

19

19 35mm print. Perforations with 'square' corners. Unidentified 'synchronised' film. Gaumont-Messter, *c.* 1904. Davide Turconi Collection, Pavia.

20

21

20 Casimir Sivan, 35mm, [*Bains de la Jetée de Pâquis, Genève*], *c.* 1896. Film Department, George Eastman House, Rochester.

21 Max Skladanowsky, 55mm (*Das boxende Känguruh*, 1895). Perforations and splices reinforced with metal studs. Film Department, George Eastman House, Rochester.

23

24

22

22 35mm print. Perforations with rounded sides. Eastman Kodak 1920 edge code (*A Daughter of Two Worlds*, James L. Young, Talmadge Film Corp., 1920). Film Department, George Eastman House, Rochester.

23 Cement splice on 35mm nitrate positive print (*Le Chevalier mystère*, Georges Méliès, Star-Film, 1899). Film Department, George Eastman House, Rochester.

24 Cement splice on 35mm negative, visible on the nitrate positive print (*Le Chevalier mystère*, Georges Méliès, Star-Film, 1899). Film Department, George Eastman House, Rochester.

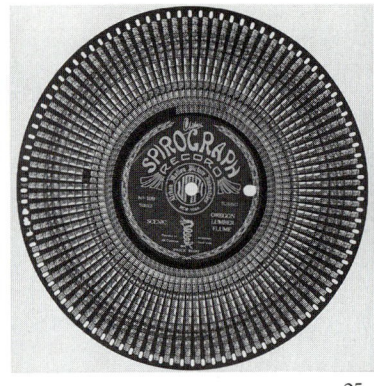

25

26

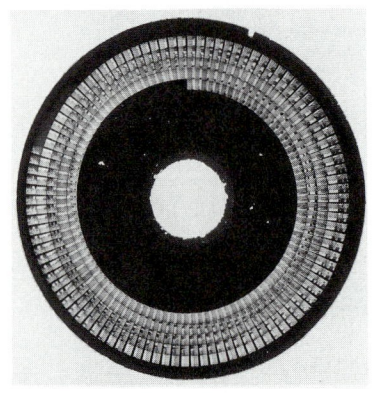

27

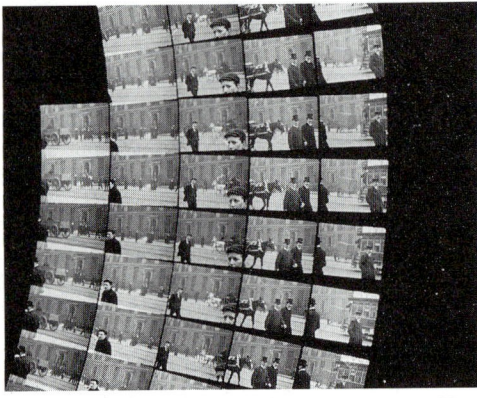

28

29

25   Charles Urban, Spirograph, 1923. (*Oregon Lumber Flume*, cat. no. 109). Eastman safety film disc (actual size, 26.7cm) with approx. 1200 frames (5.6mm x 4.1mm). Film Department, George Eastman House, Rochester.

26   Charles Urban, Spirograph, 1923. (*Oregon Lumber Flume*, cat. no. 109), detail. Film Department, George Eastman House, Rochester.

27   L. U. Kamm, Kammatograph, 1898–1900. Unidentified film (street scene). Glass plate (actual size, 30.5cm) with approx. 400 frames (8.4 x 6mm). Film Department, George Eastman House, Rochester.

28   L. U. Kamm, Kammatograph, 1898–1900. Unidentified film (street scene), detail. Film Department, George Eastman House, Rochester.

29   Technicolor process no. 2 (*The Black Pirate*, Albert Parker, Elton Corp., 1926). Negative print. Courtesy of Kevin Patton, National Film and Television Archive, London.

78

30

30 Lumière, 75mm, 1900. Courtesy of Vincent Pinel.

5
SILENT CINEMA REVISITED

All in all, the creative act is not performed by the artist alone; the spectator brings the work in contact with the external world by deciphering and interpreting its inner qualifications.

Marcel Duchamp

Film Restoration Versus Spectatorship

Spectators who know what they are doing pay attention to the content of every film they watch, but also to the technical and environmental conditions of the film's presentation. This requirement holds true in all circumstances – during an evening at the cinema, in the course of a festival, or in front of the video. However, when it is a matter of watching a film made eighty years ago, you need an extra commitment: you should try to imagine the effect of the film when it was first distributed and how that differs from the effect of the present event.

This problem can be examined from two points of view. On the one hand, you have to remember what we have called the 'internal history' of the copy – that is to say, the alterations which the print has undergone over the years. On the other hand, you have to be aware that the historical, psychological and cultural distance between our present situation and that of a 1910 audience is enormous, and that no historical inquiry will ever be able to bridge it completely. However, this is no excuse to abandon the attempt. We should try to get as close as possible to the expectations and the thinking of the people of the period when the film was made, without veiling our experience with a conceptual apparatus which distorts the object rather than bringing it closer to our understanding.

From the first point of view, knowing how to watch a silent film means realising how it has been presented to us and possibly modified in order to make it visible. At the end of Chapter 1, I reviewed some of the most typical errors made in the past by technicians and archivists in their attempts to duplicate 'original' prints. Now it is time to examine another aspect of their activity: restoration, or at least the synthesis of every modification to the 'original' print according to a consistent vision of what the film would have been originally and how it 'should' appear to a modern audience. This does not mean that every film you see in an archive is always the result of carefully conceived actions and strategies. Having to deal with staggering amounts of decaying film with usually insufficient human resources, film archives are forced to set a minimum standard for what is considered an acceptable level of intervention, and must apply this standard systematically without discussing individual cases except when they present especially challenging problems or when they are seen as being of exceptional aesthetic and historical relevance.

The restoration of a film is often the fruit of individual tenacity (or obsession); after all, that is how a vast canvas like Abel Gance's *Napoléon* (1927) has been brought back to a condition relatively close to its original one. Whatever the starting point, there are usually two aims: theoretical consistency, sometimes mislabelled as 'textual integrity', and entertainment. In various ways and to different degrees of scientific accuracy, almost every so-called film restoration has gone to one extreme or the other, or looked for a synthesis of the two.

According to the principles of consistency, a restoration is complete when the final result reflects what is supposed to have been the original concept of the film along with the incongruities and gaps shown by the copy that has come down to us. If, for example, it is certain that the second-to-last shot of a film is missing, the restorer might come to the extreme solution of pointing this out by inserting a piece of dark or blank film, perhaps describing the missing shot in an intertitle, or by inserting a production still. In that way, the spectator is informed that the object of restoration is incomplete and that this incompleteness has affected a significant part of the work. Similarly, if research shows that shots or intertitles in a 1914 film were added later, after its first commercial distribution (and if the purpose of restoration is to reconstruct the film to the form in which it was presumably shown to audiences in 1914), the additions will have to be removed. If the text of the lost intertitles has been recovered, the restorer may try to reproduce the original typeface and the original designs for the intertitles; on the other hand, he or she may do without the designs and use modern lettering. In either case it will have to be pointed out that this is a reconstruction, not a reproduction.

The sum of these precautions is meant to confirm the restorer's integrity towards the film and towards the audience to which the film will be shown. We have been deceived too often by films which we thought were conceived in a certain way but which turn out to have been altered in recent times. These alterations were made not by those who exploited the film for profit – as might have happened even many years after the first showing – but by those who had undertaken to hand down the work to posterity without having a specific competence for doing so, or an awareness of the ethical issues involved.

However, there is a problem. Don't all these precautions form a tissue of codes, emendations and interruptions which deny the non-specialist public the sheer pleasure of watching the film? And don't they deprive the informed spectator of that aesthetic pleasure which he or she might derive from a copy which might not be irreproachable from the point of view of its faithfulness to the so-called original, but which is, nevertheless, perfectly understandable in terms of plot and image quality and the meaning which both communicate to the gaze and the intellect?

The restorer who has adopted this point of view may answer that a beautiful but unfaithful copy is to be preferred over a print which conforms to a presumed 'original' version, but which in some way disrupts the very emotional impact that made the film widely acclaimed in the first place and on which its reputation is founded, or which makes this emotion unintelligible by reducing it to a sterile intellectual exercise. Saving and preserving films in order to show them as dissected corpses rather than as living works able to speak to the public of today, is – according to this philosophy of restoration – a contradiction in terms.

Telling examples of this are the three versions of David Wark Griffith's *Intolerance* (1916) which followed each other at almost yearly intervals between 1987 and 1989. The first, based on a copy from Raymond Rohauer's collection, was screened at the Avignon Festival in France with an orchestral accompaniment composed for the occasion by Antoine Duhamel and Pierre Jansen. The second was the result of a joint effort by Thames Television, film historians Kevin Brownlow and David Gill and the American composer Carl Davis, to whom we also owe a new score for the reconstruction of Gance's *Napoléon*. The third was presented by the Museum of Modern Art, New York, in collaboration with the Library of Congress in Washington.

The Museum of Modern Art restoration project started thanks to two strokes of luck: the discovery of instrumental parts of the score for the first 'official' public screening of *Intolerance* on 5 September 1916 (other unofficial screenings had been held in California in the preceding weeks), and the discovery of a notebook containing the first frame of every shot in the film in the order designated by Griffith three months before the official premiere. Thanks to these frames and the detailed instructions on the score, it was possible to work out what was apparently missing from the many copies which were then available and which had been so modified over the years that each print seemed part of an insoluble puzzle of versions, amendments and additions. The restorers decided to try to imagine what *Intolerance* might have looked like on that evening in September 1916, and to attempt what nobody had so far managed: to assemble every shot in the right order, inserting freeze frames (taken from the notebook) for the missing parts, the shot lengths being determined by the score.

When this version of *Intolerance* was shown to the public at the New York Film Festival on 2 October 1989, controversy mingled with applause. The film had substantially 'changed' from what had been known until then. New ideas and narrative digressions were recognisable; some episodes, which in earlier versions were so brief that they seemed to have been extensively cut, appeared to be better motivated; and Griffith's political opinions gained complexity and depth. Missing, in contrast, was the so-called 'pleasure of the spectator', or rather that emotional involvement which in a film like *Intolerance* can lead to genuinely thrilling moments. These were precisely the aspects which had been particularly evident in the version from the series *Thames Silents*, thanks above all to the rhetorical impact of Carl Davis's score; they also re-emerged at each showing of the Rohauer/Duhamel-Jansen version, which was enhanced by a sophisticated musical accompaniment which often helped to enhance the dramatic peaks of each episode.

The music score of the restored *Intolerance* from the Museum of Modern

Art was from Joseph Carl Breil's own score. It was written in 1916, under the supervision of Griffith himself, and respected the current conventions of musical accompaniment for silent films. It had plenty of ambition, and several quotations from material in the public domain, from Wagner to what was soon to become the American national anthem. It is not great music, but it is the music which the spectators actually heard in 1916 at some American showings of the film – nothing to do with the freely recreated scores of Davis or Duhamel and Jansen.

What option should be preferred when watching and studying silent cinema? Incomplete authenticity or artificial beauty? There is no hard and fast solution to this dilemma, but several solutions are correct and plausible, partly because they are culturally inevitable and partly because all we ask is that in each case the objectives should be clearly defined. When an institution shows a silent film which it claims to have restored, keep in mind the following possibilities:

1 The film is being shown just as it was found, with all the gaps and imperfections it had when the copy became part of the archive's collection. Here the only intervention by the technicians has been to duplicate the film onto another base and to eliminate the most noticeable defects. Even in the case of more thorough intervention, the conscientious restorer will ensure that creating a new version will not destroy the preceding one, of which at least a negative and the 'original' will be kept.

2 The film is being shown in the version which comes closest to the one that is believed to have been shown for the first time, or at a certain moment in its commercial distribution. If this cannot be achieved, the copy may be supplemented with visual information explaining the distortions or incompleteness.

3 The intentions of whoever made the film are known, and the copy restores the film to the state it should have been in before other material, historical and/or economic factors altered it. Sometimes this operation may have been carried out by the authors themselves, and if so it should be respected. Remember, however, that the result does not necessarily correspond to what the spectators of the time saw on the screen.

4 Somebody got hold of a print of the film and manipulated it in order to create a new object, with or without taking responsibility for such action. Whether we should accept or reject this intrusion depends on value judgments which change from culture to culture and with the passage of time, but it is essential that this manipulation (by an archive or an author) should not be confused with the historical identity of the object. If an unscrupulous restorer has been at work, and if his or her intervention is reversible, this identity can be recovered. When the modification or the extrapolation is intended to create a new work (as happened in 1984 with *Metropolis* by Giorgio Moroder, based on the 1926 film of the same title by Fritz Lang), it is important that the

intervention should not involve the destruction of the archive material.

However we consider the silent film being projected on the big screen or worked on at the viewing table, we should never forget that a different film was actually seen at the time of its commercial release. We can get close to this condition only if we have the rare fortune of seeing the nitrate copy; but the equipment and the auditorium, the screen, the audience's psychological expectations, the cultural and economic conditions of the time cannot be reproduced or recalled, even approximately. The 'original' print is not the same document, even though worn and incomplete, that it was in the past. On the contrary, it is simply one of the many faces the work has assumed in the course of time.

> RULE 8
> The 'original' version of a film
> is a multiple object
> fragmented into a number of different entities
> equal to the number of surviving copies.

The multiplicity of 'original' prints is a fact which we must recognise whenever we analyse a film. This awareness, however, must not become an obsession: excessive caution can at times be more paralysing and destructive than careless methodology.

The 'original' copies were usually printed on cellulose nitrate stock, whereas, in the best of cases, what we get access to is a 35mm acetate or polyester copy. Apart from the fact that any reproduction necessarily involves a loss of information, we know that the clarity and the contrast which were typical of a nitrate copy can be imitated but never reproduced perfectly on a different base. We also know that the 'original' prints were often in colour, while many of those available to us are in black and white. If they are not, it almost always means that the colour has been reproduced by modern techniques (experiments in colouring copies by the techniques of the silent period are admirable, though rare, exceptions), and it is certain that these techniques are as yet unable to reproduce with absolute fidelity the subtle chromatic variations and light effects of some 'original' prints. But complaining because the best restored copy is shown through a projector which, even though it has a three-blade shutter and is able to run at variable speeds, does not use carbon lighting, reminds us of Theodor W. Adorno's comment about the 'resentful listener': some orchestral scores by Johann Sebastian Bach required, among other instruments, a hunting horn whose performance was so uneven that it could not be played with ease even by a proficient musician. What sense would it make, then, nowadays, to insert an early eighteenth-century hunting horn into a performance for original instruments? In our case, this would be like demanding a projector which could not guarantee the steadiness of the projected image.

The progressive deterioration of the film after repeated showings was taken for granted by the pioneers of cinema and by the industry which replaced them a decade later, and was even considered desirable inasmuch as producers and cinema owners were obliged to return or destroy them after use. Cinema has always been an art of the ephemeral. It still is so today, and it was even more so in 1905, when the demand for new moving images had become so intense that films which could no longer be commercially exploited were thrown away without a second thought. The operetta scores by Jacques Offenbach, today considered of great historical and aesthetic value, suffered a similar fate: when a certain piece of music had gone out of the repertory, the score could be used to wrap fish in the market of Les Halles. That some of these old films have survived, and can still be seen, is a miracle in itself. Their survival was neither foreseen nor believed to be desirable. As we have seen, the differences between these films and their copies of today are numerous and far from superficial. Recognition of these differences does not mean, however, that we should ignore their implications; after all, we know that many of the statues from ancient Greece were brightly coloured, yet the sculptors who worked on the temples of the Acropolis are judged great artists even though their work is now identified with the whiteness of marble. The same goes for classical Greek tragedy. It was certainly not performed originally as it is performed today, but it is not rejected as 'false' by modern specialists because of that.

In recovering silent cinema, as in recovering all images from the past, the search for authenticity must be carried out in the light of what is feasible. The projection of a silent film with an improvised musical accompaniment is no more 'true' or close to historical accuracy than a screening in absolute silence. There is no doubt, however, that piano improvisations were the rule in small suburban cinemas and that – strictly speaking – a show with live music is more authentic than a projection in an auditorium where all you can hear is specialists murmuring to each other while taking notes. The difference is that an ordinary spectator who has seen a silent film with music may wish to come back and see another.

Similarly, it is right that silent films which were originally in colour should be restored and presented in colour; but colour is an element which gives value to the image, not a lacquer which veils the contrasts and suffocates the chiaroscuro. During the last fifteen years film restoration has undergone a spectacular evolution which will, one hopes, continue at the same rate. However, if available techniques still cannot eliminate altogether the current short-comings, the 'original' image one aims at might as well be similar to one derived from a nitrate negative, mostly in black and white. Since it is a duplicate, it is not unfair to compare it – at least from this point of view – to a photograph of a painting: the authors of many art history books prefer a good half-tone reproduction to one in garish colours. The choice made by many archives in favour of black-and-white duplicates is also dictated by the relative instability of colour film stock currently in use. This does not mean that we should abandon altogether the idea of showing silent films with the colours approximating as closely as possible those of the 'originals', but a silent film which has been superficially tarted up is not the restorer's ideal object, nor is it a delight to the eyes of the audience.

The Ethics of Research

One learns the rules of intellectual work by observing how research grows and evolves, by recognising one's own and other people's mistakes and by adopting a respectful attitude towards those who will use the work. In part, one can demonstrate this respect by refusing to use short cuts or to resort to methods which sacrifice the value of the result to the ease with which it can be achieved. Remember this when studying a silent film, because the temptation to interpret it according to familiar precepts is strong, at times hard to resist. However, resist we must. Although the early cinema requires methods of analysis which are compatible with it, at times you must adopt an attitude of both detachment and identification, being wary of passively adopting present-day criteria for the aesthetic and ideological evaluation of a visual message presented in the form of projected images. The reason why people so often laugh when watching a silent film, even a drama, is that the narrative conventions, the visual and verbal signals of expression, the techniques for reproducing reality and the abstractions of meaning are so markedly different from our own. It seems natural to regard them with a mixture of condescension and superiority, as in the 1950s one regarded elderly people who expressed amazement at their first sight of a television.

We should try to identify with a public for whom the moving photographic image was, and continued to be for several years, a real miracle, and with the rhetorical strategies being used at the time to communicate the meaning and the possibilities of film. Today, we take for granted that a hectic montage of shots belonging to different contexts should be immediately understandable. But can we really imagine how difficult and deeply felt the decision to place one piece of film next to another in order to produce the effect of continuous action may have been?

The average length of a feature film is now about ninety minutes, but there was a time when cinema owners resolutely opposed showing a story which lasted that long. Fifteen minutes was believed to be more than enough. Increasing the duration of a story to thirty minutes, and then to forty-five, was a difficult task achieved only after harsh conflicts between directors, distributors and production companies. At times, films from the beginning of the century, lasting no longer than fifteen minutes, today seem so packed with action and incident that they are very difficult to follow, but the 1908 audience was so used to it that they noticed with great precision details of gesture and décor which are barely recognisable to us.

The silent cinema's first audiences perceived the sequence of time differently from us. It was far from rare – and for at least seven years, from 1900 to 1906, it was common practice – to show two consecutive actions without worrying about establishing a direct visual connection between them: the causal connection was judged quite sufficient. This pattern of representing time is based on the concept of time lapse: an action was shown underlining its possible consequences, and then the next shot followed, showing the consequences already in operation, even if the action does not start exactly where it ended in the preceding image. The passing of time was taken for granted; therefore it was not shown.

31 Violet tinting. Unidentified film.

32 Sepia toning. Unidentified film.

33 Sepia toning on red tinting. Unidentified film.

34 Brown toning on blue tinting. Unidentified film.

35 Blue mordanting. Unidentified film.

36 Red mordanting on blue tinting. Unidentified film.

Plates 31–36 are taken from *Le film vierge Pathé* (Paris: Établissements Pathé-Cinéma, 1926), Tables IV–VI (frame samples Nos 55, 71 *bis*, 88, 83, 90, 98).

37   Hand-coloured and stencil-coloured print. Unidentified film (Urban–Eclipse *c.*, 1907 [*The Abducted Gypsy*]). Film Department, George Eastman House, Rochester.

38   Stencil-coloured print (Pathécolor system, also known as *au pochoir* colouring) (*Fée aux pigeons*, Pathé, April–May 1906). Paolo Cherchi Usai Collection.

39   Hand-coloured and stencil-coloured print (*L'écrin du Radjah*, Pathé, April–May 1906). Davide Turconi Collection, Pavia.

40   Turquoise tinting, (*Firenze*, Milano Film, 1913). The 'stencil' Eastman edge code is visible on the right, between the perforations. Nederlands Filmmuseum, Amsterdam.

41

42

41 Green toning (*Dödsritten under Cirkuskupolen*, Georg af Klercker, Svenska Biografteatern, 1912). Film Department, George Eastman House, Rochester.

42 Stencil-colouring on toning. Unidentified Gaumont film, *c.* 1908 (*Roi Midas*). Davide Turconi Collection, Pavia.

43

44

43 Blue toning. Unidentified film, possibly Gaumont, 1907 (German titles: *Braut des Freiwilligen* or *1870*). Davide Turconi Collection, Pavia.

44 Kodachrome process, *c.* 1922. The edge code is visible on the right. Film Department, George Eastman House, Rochester.

45 Handschiegl process (also known as Wyckoff-DeMille process) (*The Ten Commandments*, Cecil B. DeMille, Famous Players-Lasky Corp., 1923), reel 4. Film Department, George Eastman House, Rochester.

46 William Friese-Greene three-colour system, *c.* 1909. Film Department, George Eastman House, Rochester.

47 Technicolor process no. 3 (*Redskin*, Victor Schertzinger, Paramount, 1929). Film Department, George Eastman House, Rochester.

48 Chronochrome Gaumont three-colour process (*Paris Fashion. Latest Spring Hats* [US title], 1913). Black-and-white panchromatic film, to be projected through a triple lens unit with colour filters. Film Department, George Eastman House, Rochester.

A parallel case is the use of temporal overlap. A series of events is described and then, in the next shot, some actions from the previous shot are repeated from another point of view, reinforcing the continuity between the two segments. As time went by, these techniques fell into disuse. In the end, they came to be considered editing 'mistakes' (unless they occurred in an experimental film). However, for almost a decade, such narrative devices were considered perfectly legitimate, at least until Griffith and his contemporaries developed what we call today 'continuity' editing.

These are only a few examples among many. The same holds true for all instances of 'unfamiliar' devices: they should not be judged according to today's criteria. They did not 'anticipate' more sophisticated techniques, nor were they 'late' compared with more contemporary stylistic parameters. It has taken years to stop people calling this period of cinema 'primitive', with its heavily pejorative connotations. Now and then, some scholars revive this label, claiming to have found new reasons to justify it. But before we follow their example, let us consider what definitions are actually for. Some help us to place a technique, a visual constant or a narrative model along interweaving lines of evolution which often contradict and cancel each other, and then re-emerge in a different form. Others force the film into straitjackets modelled on reductive categorisations, fashionable theories or tenuous intuitions. To make films say what one wants them to say, as if they were objects one can manipulate at will, is a petty verbal exercise carried out at the expense of images which have been ripped out of the context which gave them life. Since the early cinema and the silent cinema in general have become subjects of academic interest, they have given rise to illuminating theoretical constructions, but also to conceptual scaffolding which has no justification other than its own existence.

When countering this danger, we run the risk of applying a remedy that is worse than the original evil – that is to say, we could turn 'historical fact' into a fetish to ward off verbal somersaults and mental confusion. However, brandishing this fetish, with its high concentration of simplistic positivism, turns silent cinema into a dry catalogue of names, dates, patents and events, mercilessly yoked together into annals totally devoid of life. In the past, this cataloguing syndrome has given rise to a paradoxical search for technical records: who made the first tracking shot, which is the first full-length film, which was the first camera capable of holding more than forty metres of film, who shot the first cinema footage through a microscope?

Underpinning this collector's attitude to source research is a double misunderstanding. On the one hand, it is believed that putting pieces of information in neatly serried ranks is the essence of historical research, and that these pieces of information should be 'confirmed' by documentary proof whose mere existence is mistaken for their relevance. On the other hand, it is implicitly claimed that research on silent cinema should exclude any kind of aesthetic or political judgment on the works created with those machines, or by the men and women and production structures which made them possible. Thus a dual negative effect is produced in the name of 'historical accuracy': on the one hand, silent cinema is left to the most gratuitous speculation; on the other, it is treated as an object of study comparable to naval engineering or to the tobacco trade.

However, we are talking about objects with an intrinsic aesthetic and cultural value. All silent films are such, from *Intolerance* to the humblest chase comedies. That the creators of the latter were generally motivated by intentions which do not wholly correspond to the kind of things usually analysed in books of art history does not prevent us from comparing their works to the music, painting and literature of the time when they were made. It is right, therefore, that the Musée d'Orsay in Paris, which is devoted to the arts of the late 19th and early 20th centuries, has dedicated exhibition space to silent cinema. Doing otherwise would have been to deny what has been repeated since the days of critics and theoreticians such as Louis Delluc and Ricciotto Canudo, but which is too often taken for granted without putting the idea into practice: cinema, as a whole, is an aesthetic phenomenon.

Such are the principles. But how do we put them into practice without betraying the object's specific nature? I have already made some formal suggestions about the principles to be followed. Calling them 'rules' and setting them out in such a way that they stand out on the page is not authoritarian didacticism. On the contrary, it is intended to stress their problematic nature. The other suggestions scattered throughout this book are mostly pieces of advice which we would do well to remember whenever a project seems to be running along the rails of predictability, or convenience, or when we fall prey to the ambition to say new things at any cost. It is inevitable that from time to time laziness gets the better of us, but the quality of our research and our pleasure as spectators would be lastingly enhanced by the ability to apply the following principles systematically:

1 Whenever possible, see the greatest possible number of prints of the same film, especially if the film is the subject of a case study or of a well defined theoretical or historical hypothesis. Always ensure that the notes on the titles you consult are full and detailed. Clearly, it is often impossible to comment on every print shot by shot, but sometimes the important differences between two prints are also the least striking, and a set of good viewing notes – in addition to well trained powers of concentration – is often a decisive resource for making the most exciting and unexpected discoveries.

2 When consulting information sources, never trust data implicitly. This is equally true for film credits, actors' faces, primary and secondary sources – even contemporary magazines can be wrong. Reasonable explanations, contributory circumstances, causal links which seem perfectly plausible can lead to resounding errors in judgment. The opposite is also true: things that appear inconsistent but are not, coincidences which are believed impossible, dates and lengths of films that 'do not fit', styles that seem too 'old-fashioned' or too 'advanced' for the time.

In their memoirs, film directors of the silent era could sometimes exaggerate their merits, or mix them up with other people's, precisely as happens today, and their attitude was often magnified by the journalists who interviewed them. A certain distortion of the facts was also typical of some producers who were in the habit of attributing to themselves the authorship of other people's work. We are reminded of a warning to researchers dear to a great Italian mentor, the film historian Davide Turconi: Studying the history of cinema is like venturing into quicksands. One wrong premise, one misunderstood or unverified piece of information is enough to change research into a tangle of false trails and mistakes from which there is no way out.

3 Part of the time spent visiting a film archive should be devoted to exploring the catalogue. If this is allowed, it can lead to the discovery of recently acquired titles or titles unknown to us. Time should be allowed for assessing any supplementary information about known copies (donors, date of finding, to which specific collection the film belongs).

4 Archive rules permitting, it is always best to consult the 'original' print of the film we are studying. However difficult it may be to get access to nitrate copies, for those who watch silent films for research, and who want to make sure that their hypotheses are well founded, a quick look at the original print can dispel many doubts. Therefore it is sometimes useful to explain to those who are in charge of preservation that the purpose of the request is not to project the print, but, for example, simply to look at it to check the inscriptions along the edges of a Pathé film (see Appendix III) or the shape of the splices in an alternate editing sequence.

5 Non-fiction films deserve the same attention and respect accorded to fiction films. This advice would be superfluous if documentaries and news footage were privileged objects of aesthetic and historical research, but they are not: attention is focused mostly on fiction cinema. This seems easier to analyse because it is 'narrative' (as if 'narrating' concerned only what belongs to the world of the imagination) and more suitable as a testing ground for theories derived from literary practice and for the cult of the auteur and of the 'great performer'. And yet it is well known – and worth repeating – that many technical and stylistic resources which cinema acquired over its first thirty years arose and developed within this galaxy of images overlooked by most film histories.

6 Many films still have no name. This is inevitable. Some of them became part of collections when they were no longer complete, which can make it hard to find their titles, directors or production companies. This is also their misfortune, since archives usually do not like restoring anonymous films. When they must allocate money for restoration, curators want to be sure that the funds have been spent well, on 'important' films which are in demand from researchers and appreciated by the public as well as by the institutions that make the necessary funds available. As I said in Chapter 2, the imperative of film archives is 'to restore everything', but, since resources are always limited, harsh decisions on selection have to be made.

Unidentified films pay the price for this, and treasures of incalculable value lie buried for decades and disappear through decay before somebody is able to bring them back to light. Some institutions at the forefront of the archive movement try to restore these films too, though, and we can help them by supplementing our planned viewing with a number of unidentified prints belonging to the period we feel we know best.

7 The study of silent cinema covers a vast field of research. It can give rise to an enthusiasm for conquest, and to the understandable euphoria of thinking we have made a discovery at every corner. Sometimes it really is a significant discovery, and sometimes the person who makes it is clever enough to turn the find into an effective career device. However, before we announce the discovery of an essential fragment of information missing from the common heritage, we would do well to check whether somebody has not already found it, perhaps half a century ago, perhaps using inaccurate methods and without backing the claim with footnotes and quotations, but with the right ideas in the right place.

Film studies are subject – perhaps even more so than other fields of knowledge – to a merciless law of evolution, summarised by Rudolf Arnheim in his *New Essays on the Psychology of Art*:

> A discipline grows like a tree, one on which the nature and function of every new twig is determined by its place in the whole. Each contribution justifies itself by addressing a question that the profession has put on the agenda at that time. Later workers along the same line dutifully cite their forerunners by name and date, with the implication that the passage of time equals progress, and that the pioneers of today stand on the shoulders of yesterday's dwarfs. Everybody profits from the safety of the totem pole.

Scholars once responsible for groundbreaking research on silent cinema are remembered today with a dismissive attitude, easily discerned between the lines of the usual admiring testimonials. They are blamed for having tried to write a whole history of the cinema by themselves, they are judged by their 'impressionist' methods of analysis, and we often hear complaints that some controversial statement has not been supported with the necessary documentation. In other words, these predecessors are accused of not having acted with the hindsight with which we latecomers are blessed, and of failing to use the precious primary sources now no longer available to us. We forget that, thanks to their efforts, we have at our disposal (due to the collective, less individualistic though no less competitive character of current film studies) material which is just as precious and which none of them ever had the chance to see.

Film History Pursued by Other Means
Those who watch silent films with a more than occasional interest possess certain books which are frequently consulted but rarely read from cover to cover. The names of Georges Sadoul, Jerzy Toeplitz, Jean Mitry, Jacques Deslandes and Rachael Low are the ones that crop up most frequently. Quite often, when we turn to these authors for confirmation of the importance of the

data we think we have brought to light, we are left feeling somehow disappointed and surprised, as if the trust we placed in them had been betrayed. But it is one thing to recognise the shortcomings of those who went before us, and another to measure their accomplishments by the standards used in some antiquarian bookshops, where the pride of owning an old magazine or a rare book is in proportion to a lack of interest in its contents.

Some of these books and magazines, however filled with defects they may be, are evidence of how the silent cinema survived the extremes of nostalgic celebration and the indifference of the 'high-art' milieu. Reading these documents with caution does not mean taking the risk of being contaminated by obsolete methodologies and outdated ideas. On the contrary, it means going back to the noblest origins of film historiography and understanding why the critical reputation of certain authors, their films and the styles they represented, has determined the survival of some works and the disappearance of others.

The tendency to confuse detailed description and quantification with scientific method is the result of an illusion which has affected silent cinema studies for some time, but which is accompanied more and more frequently by what Arnheim calls 'the fashionable infatuation that burdens words with unreasonable responsibilities'. Nobody can, or wants to, prevent an object of study being transformed into statistical data or evidence in support of existing theories, but those who do this have the duty to point out that no detailed description of a film – even when it is dissected with the sharpest conceptual device – is an adequate substitute for the actual viewing of it.

The one thing which should never be questioned, whatever conceptual tool we adopt, is the guarantee that films are given a chance to speak for themselves. While being projected, films can confirm or deny the ideas and causal connections we may have suggested in order to draw out deeper layers of their meaning. A film can tell a contemporary spectator much more than its creators meant to imply: each image is the crystallisation of a society and a culture, and because of our position in history we may know the consequences of these momentary images, and maybe understand better the circumstances which shaped them. But we must not exploit this knowledge. There is a gap separating the producer of silent motion pictures, the contemporary viewers of these images and today's audiences. We may well attempt to decrease this gap, but the fractures and absences are very deep in the case of silent cinema: too many material and cultural circumstances separate us from it, and our patterns of perception of moving images have changed too much in the meantime. Herein lies the fascinating challenge of studying silent cinema: both the greatest discipline and the greatest imagination are needed in order to bring back to life something which is relatively close to us in time. It is closer than prehistoric art or the music of ancient Egypt, but it can be no less mysterious and elusive.

To prevent this historical and psychological distance from becoming unbridgeable, I have recommended watching silent films in a form which is closest to the original – that is to say, as a projection of light through a semi-transparent photographic base. One may insist that other systems are more practical and less expensive than film. This point of view is as acceptable as examining the photograph of a painting instead of the actual canvas, or being introduced to a music score by means of a recorded performance, or encountering a work of architecture through drawings or models. But sooner or later we will have to take the next step, and attend the concert hall, walk through the cathedral at different times of day, observe the painting at close quarters, see frames of a film projected in quick succession on a white surface. The sooner we decide to do so, the better we shall understand why cinema came into being and how, among the many possible patterns of evolution, its existence has become entwined with that of millions of people who, thanks to it, have laughed and suffered, followed their dreams and drawn in the dark, in front of the screen, a new image of the world.

APPENDIX I

FILM MEASUREMENT TABLES

35mm		projection speed (frames per second)					16mm	
metres	feet	16	18	20	22	24	metres	feet
				running time				
0.3	1	1″	1″	1″	1″	1″	0.1	0.4
0.7	2	2″	2″	2″	2″	1″	0.3	1.0
1.0	3	3″	3″	2″	2″	2″	0.4	1.3
1.2	4	4″	4″	3″	3″	3″	0.5	1.6
1.5	5	5″	4″	4″	4″	3″	0.6	2.0
1.8	6	6″	5″	5″	4″	4″	0.7	2.4
2.0	7	7″	6″	6″	5″	5″	0.8	2.7
2.3	8	8″	7″	6″	6″	5″	0.9	3.0
2.7	9	9″	8″	7″	7″	5″	1.0	3.3
3.0	10	10″	9″	8″	7″	7″	1.2	4.0
3.3	11	11″	10″	9″	8″	7″	1.3	4.4
3.8	12	12″	11″	10″	9″	8″	1.5	5.0
4.0	13	13″	12″	10″	9″	9″	1.6	5.3
4.3	14	14″	13″	11″	10″	9″	1.7	5.6
4.6	15	15″	13″	12″	11″	10″	1.8	6.0
5.0	16	16″	14″	13″	12″	11″	2.0	6.5
5.1	17	17″	15″	14″	12″	11″	2.0	6.6
5.3	18	18″	16″	14″	13″	12″	2.1	7.0
5.8	19	19″	17″	15″	14″	13″	2.3	7.6
6.0	20	20″	18″	16″	14″	13″	2.4	7.8
6.1	20	20″	18″	16″	15″	13″	2.4	8.0
6.4	21	21″	19″	17″	15″	14″	2.6	8.4
6.7	22	22″	20″	18″	16″	15″	2.7	8.8
7.0	23	23″	21″	18″	17″	15″	2.7	9.0
7.3	24	24″	22″	19″	17″	16″	2.9	9.6
7.6	25	25″	22″	20″	18″	17″	3.0	9.9
7.6	25	25″	22″	20″	18″	17″	3.1	10
8.0	26	26″	23″	21″	19″	18″	3.3	11
8.2	27	27″	24″	22″	20″	18″	3.3	11
8.5	28	28″	25″	22″	20″	19″	3.4	11
8.8	29	29″	26″	23″	21″	19″	3.5	12
9.0	30	30″	27″	24″	22″	20″	3.6	12

		projection speed (frames per second)						
35mm		16	18	20	22	24	16mm	
metres	feet			running time			metres	feet
10.0	33	33″	30″	26″	24″	22″	4.0	13
10.7	35	35″	31″	28″	25″	23″	4.3	14
12.2	40	40″	36″	32″	29″	26″	4.9	16
12.5	41	41″	36′	32″	30″	27″	5.0	16
13.7	45	45″	41″	36″	32″	30″	5.5	18
15.0	49	49″	44″	39″	36″	32″	6.0	20
15.2	50	50″	45″	40″	36″	33″	6.1	20
16.8	55	55″	50″	44″	40″	36″	6.7	22
18.3	60	1′00″	54″	48″	43″	40″	7.3	24
19.8	65	1′05″	59″	52″	47″	43″	7.9	26
20.0	66	1′05″	59″	53″	48″	44″	8.0	26
21.3	70	1′10″	1′03″	56″	50″	46″	8.5	28
22.9	75	1′15″	1′08″	1′00″	54″	50″	9.2	30
24.4	80	1′20″	1′12″	1′04″	58″	53″	9.8	32
25.0	82	1′21″	1′13″	1′05″	1′00″	55″	10.0	33
25.9	85	1′25″	1′17″	1′08″	1′01″	56″	10.4	34
27.4	90	1′30″	1′21″	1′12″	1′05″	59″	11.0	36
28.9	95	1′35″	1′25″	1′16″	1′08″	1′03″	11.6	38
30.0	98	1′37″	1′27″	1′18″	1′11″	1′05″	11.9	39
30.5	100	1′40″	1′29″	1′19″	1′12″	1′07″	12.2	40
35.0	116	1′55″	1′43″	1′32″	1′24″	1′17″	14.1	46
38.1	125	2′05″	1′51″	1′39″	1′30″	1′24″	15.2	50
40.0	131	2′10″	1′56″	1′44″	1′35″	1′27″	16.0	52
45.0	147	2′26″	2′11″	1′57″	1′46″	1′38″	17.9	59
45.7	150	2′30″	2′15″	2′00″	1′48″	1′40″	18.3	60
50.0	164	2′43″	2′25″	2′11″	1′59″	1′49″	20.0	66
53.3	175	2′55″	2′37″	2′20″	2′06″	1′56″	21.3	70
55.0	180	2′59″	2′40″	2′25″	2′11″	2′00″	21.9	72
60.0	197	3′16″	2′54″	2′38″	2′23″	2′11″	24.0	79
61.0	200	3′20″	2′58″	2′40″	2′25″	2′13″	24.4	80
62.5	205	3′25″	3′02″	2′44″	2′29″	2′17″	25.0	82
65.0	216	3′35″	3′12″	2′53″	2′37″	2′24″	26.3	86
68.6	225	3′45″	3′22″	3′00″	2′42″	2′29″	27.4	90
70.0	230	3′49″	3′24″	3′04″	2′47″	2′33″	28.0	92
75.0	246	4′05″	3′38″	3′16″	2′59″	2′44″	30.0	98
76.2	250	4′10″	3′41″	3′19″	3′01″	2′47″	30.5	100
80.0	262	4′21″	3′52″	3′29″	3′10″	2′54″	31.9	105
82.3	270	4′30″	4′00″	3′35″	3′16″	3′00″	32.9	108
83.8	275	4′34″	4′08″	3′40″	3′18″	3′02″	33.5	110
85.0	286	4′45″	4′13″	3′48″	3′28″	3′10″	34.9	114
90.0	295	4′54″	4′22″	3′55″	3′35″	3′16″	36.9	118
91.4	300	5′00″	4′27″	3′59″	3′38″	3′20″	37.0	120
95.0	316	5′15″	4′40″	4′12″	3′50″	3′30″	38.5	126
100.0	328	5′27″	4′51″	4′22″	3′59″	3′38″	40.0	131
106.7	350	5′49″	5′15″	4′40″	4′12″	3′51″	42.7	140
121.9	400	6′40″	5′56″	5′19″	4′51″	4′27″	48.8	160
125.0	410	6′50″	6′04″	5′24″	4′58″	4′35″	50.0	164
137.2	450	7′29″	6′45″	6′00″	5′24″	4′57″	55.0	180
150.0	492	8′11″	7′16″	6′33″	5′57″	5′28″	60.0	197
152.4	500	8′19″	7′23″	6′39″	6′03″	5′33″	61.0	200
167.6	550	9′09″	8′15″	7′20″	6′36″	6′03″	67.0	220

			projection speed (frames per second)					
35mm		*16*	*18*	*20*	*22*	*24*	*16mm*	
metres	*feet*			*running time*			*metres*	*feet*
182.9	600	10′	9′00″	8′00″	7′12″	6′36″	77.2	253
198.1	650	11′	9′45″	8′40″	7′48″	7′09″	79.2	260
200.0	656	11′	9′50″	8′44″	7′57″	7′17″	80.0	262
213.3	700	12′	10′	9′20″	8′24″	7′42″	85.3	280
228.6	750	12′	11′	10′	9′00″	8′15″	91.4	300
243.8	800	13′	12′	11′	9′36″	8′48″	97.5	320
250.0	820	14′	12′	11′	9′56″	9′06″	99.9	328
250.1	820	14′	12′	11′	10′	9′09″	100.0	328
259.1	850	14′	13′	11′	10′	9′21″	103.6	340
266.7	875	15′	13′	12′	11′	10′	106.7	350
274.3	900	15′	13′	12′	11′	10′	109.7	360
281.9	925	15′	14′	12′	11′	10′	112.8	370
289.6	950	16′	14′	13′	11′	11′	115.8	380
297.2	975	17′	14′	13′	12′	11′	118.9	390
300.0	984	17′	15′	13′	12′	11′	120.0	394
304.8	1000	17′	15′	13′	12′	11′	121.9	400
350.0	1148	19′	17′	15′	14′	13′	140.0	459
381.1	1250	21′	19′	16′	15′	14′	152.4	500
400.0	1312	22′	19′	17′	16′	15′	160.0	525
450.0	1476	25′	22′	20′	18′	16′	179.9	590
457.2	1500	25′	22′	20′	18′	16′	182.9	600
500.0	1640	27′	24′	22′	20′	18′	199.9	656
500.1	1641	27′	24′	22′	20′	18′	200.0	656
533.4	1750	29′	26′	23′	21′	19′	213.4	700
548.6	1800	30′	27′	24′	22′	20′	219.4	720
579.1	1900	32′	28′	25′	23′	21′	231.6	760
600.0	1969	33′	29′	26′	24′	22′	240.1	788
609.6	2000	33′	30′	27′	24′	22′	243.8	800
625.0	2051	34′	30′	27′	25′	23′	250.0	820
685.8	2250	37′	33′	30′	27′	25′	274.3	900
700.0	2297	38′	34′	31′	28′	26′	280.0	919
750.0	2461	41′	36′	33′	30′	27′	300.0	984
762.2	2500	42′	37′	34′	30′	28′	304.8	1000
800.0	2625	44′	39′	35′	32′	29′	320.0	1050
900.0	2953	49′	44′	39′	36′	33′	360.0	1181
914.4	3000	50′	44′	40′	36′	33′	365.8	1200
990.6	3250	54′	48′	43′	39′	36′	396.2	1300
1000.0	3281	55′	49′	44′	40′	36′	400.0	1312
1066.7	3500	58′	52′	47′	42′	39′	426.7	1400
1142.9	3750	62′	56′	50′	45′	42′	457.2	1500
1219.2	4000	67′	59′	53′	48′	44′	487.7	1600
1250.0	4101	68′	61′	55′	50′	46′	500.0	1640
1295.3	4250	71′	63′	57′	51′	47′	518.1	1700
1371.5	4500	75′	67′	60′	54′	50′	548.6	1800
1447.7	4750	79′	70′	63′	57′	52′	579.1	1900
1500.0	4922	82′	73′	66′	60′	55′	600.0	1969
1524.0	5000	83′	74′	67′	61′	56′	609.6	2000
1600.1	5250	87′	78′	70′	63′	58′	640.0	2100
1676.3	5500	91′	82′	73′	66′	61′	670.5	2200
1752.5	5750	96′	85′	77′	70′	64′	701.0	2300
1828.8	6000	100′	89′	80′	73′	67′	731.5	2400

| 35mm | | projection speed (frames per second) | | | | | 16mm | |
metres	feet	16	18	20	22	24	metres	feet
				running time				
1904.9	6250	104'	93'	83'	76'	69'	762.0	2500
1981.1	6500	108'	96'	87'	79'	72'	792.4	2600
2000.0	6562	109'	97'	87'	80'	73'	800.0	2625
2057.3	6750	112'	100'	90'	82'	75'	822.9	2700
2133.6	7000	117'	104'	93'	85'	78'	853.4	2800
2209.7	7250	120'	108'	96'	88'	80'	883.9	2900
2285.9	7500	125'	111'	100'	91'	83'	914.4	3000
2362.1	7750	129'	115'	103'	93'	86'	944.8	3100
2438.4	8000	133'	118'	107'	97'	89'	975.4	3200
2500.0	8203	137'	121'	109'	99'	91'	1000.0	3281
2590.7	8500	142'	126'	113'	103'	94'	1036.3	3400
2743.2	9000	150'	133'	120'	109'	100'	1097.3	3600
2895.5	9500	159'	141'	126'	115'	105'	1158.2	3800
3000.0	9843	164'	146'	131'	119'	109'	1200.0	3937
3048.0	10000	167'	148'	133'	121'	111'	1219.2	4000

Note: Running times above ten minutes are rounded to the minute.

An alternative solution for calculating screening times is to use the following table (valid only for lengths expressed in metres):

frames per second	35mm	16mm
24	27.36	10.97
22	25.08	10.03
20	22.80	9.12
18	20.52	8.21
16	18.24	7.29

For example, in order to establish the screening time of a 16mm print of 219.4 meters at 24 frames per second, the equation is:

$$219.4 \div 10.97 = 20 \text{ minutes}$$

APPENDIX II

FILM ARCHIVES

The following is a list of the institutions belonging to the Fédération Internationale des Archives du Film (FIAF). The directory, last updated on 18 June 1994, lists all members regardless of the status (associates, full and provisional members) subsequent to the redefinitions agreed at the Forty-Seventh Congress of FIAF (Athens, 17–25 April 1991). The names of the representatives to whom requests for access to material should be addressed, along with telephone, telex and fax numbers, and each archive's telegraphic address, can be obtained by writing to the institutions concerned or to the FIAF head office, 190 rue Franz Merjay, 1180 Brussels, Belgium. A comprehensive list of the 577 FIAF and non-FIAF institutions can be found in Wolfgang Klaue (ed.), *World Directory of Moving Image and Sound Archives* (Munich: K. G. Saur, 1993).

ALBANIA
Arkivi Shteteror i Filmit i RPS te Shqiperise (Archive d'État du Film de la RPS d'Albanie)   Rruga Aleksander Moisiu 76, Tirana

ANGOLA
Cinemateca Nacional de Angola   Largo Luther King 4, Luanda (mailing address: Caixa Postal 3512)

ARGENTINA
Fundación Cinemateca Argentina   Corrientes 2092 piso 2º, 1045 Buenos Aires

AUSTRALIA
National Film and Sound Archive   McCoy Circuit, Acton, ACT 2601, Canberra (mailing address: GPO Box 2002, Canberra, ACT 2601)

The State Film Archives of Western Australia   Alexander Library Building, Perth Cultural Centre, Perth, WA 6000

Color Film Pty Ltd   Attn. Mr Glenn Eley, 35 Missenden Road, Camperdown, NSW 2050

AUSTRIA
Österreichisches Filmarchiv   Rauhensteingasse 5, A-1010 Vienna

Österreichisches Filmmuseum   Augustinerstrasse 1, A-1010 Vienna

Bangladesh Film Archive Ministry of Information, Block No 3, Ganobhaban, Sher-E-Bangla Nagar, Dhaka-1207

Cinémathèque Royale/Koninklijk Filmarchief 23 rue Ravenstein, 1000 Brussels

Cinemateca Boliviana Calle Pichincha Esq. Indaburo, La Paz (mailing address: Casilla 9933, La Paz)

Cinemateca do Museu de Arte Moderna Av. Infante Dom Henrique 85, 20021 Rio de Janeiro, RJ (mailing address: Caixa Postal 44, 20000 Rio de Janeiro)

Cinemateca Brasileira Rua Volkswagen, 04344 São Paulo, SP (mailing address: Caixa Postal 12.900, 04092 São Paulo)

Bulgarska Nacionalna Filmoteka ul. Gourko 36, 1000 Sofia

La Cinémathèque Québécoise 335 Boulevard de Maisonneuve Est, Montréal H2X 1K1

Moving Image and Sound Archives/Division des Archives Audio-Visuelles 395 Wellington Street, Ottawa K1A ON3

Zhongguo Dianying Ziliaoguan (China Film Archive) Xin Wai Dajie 25B, Beijing

Cinemateca Distrital Carrera 7a no 22–79, Bogotá DE

Fundación Patrimonio Filmico Colombiano Carrera 13 no 13–24 Piso 9° Auditorio, Bogotá DE

Kinoteka Hrvatske/Arkiv Hrvatske Savska 131 41000 Zagreb

Český Filmovỹ Ústav/Národni Filmovỹ Archiv Narodni 40, POB 1001, 110 00 Prague 1

Cinemateca de Cuba Calle 23, no 1155, Vedado, Havana

Det Danske Filmmuseum Store Søndervoldstraede, 4, DK-1419 Copenhagen K (mailing address: Postbox 2158, DK-1016 Copenhagen K)

Cinemateca Nacional del Ecuador Av. 6 de Diciembre 794 y Tarqui, Quito (mailing address: Casa de la Cultura Ecuadoriana, Casilla 17–01–3520, Quito)

Al-Archive al-Kawmy lil-Film (National Film Archive) c/o Egyptian Film Center, City of Arts, Pyramids Avenue, El Guîza

Suomen Elokuva-Arkisto Pursimiehenkatu 29–31, 00151 Helsinki (mailing address: PL 177, 00151 Helsinki)

Archives du Film/Centre National de la Cinématographie 7bis rue Alexandre Turpault, 78390 Bois d'Arcy

Cinémathèque de Toulouse 12 rue du Faubourg Bonnefoy, 31500 Toulouse

La Cinémathèque Française 29 rue du Colisée, 75008 Paris

Musée du Cinéma de Lyon 69 rue Jean Jaurès, 69100 Villeurbanne

Musée Départemental Albert Kahn Quai du 4 Septembre, 10, 92100 Boulogne-Billancourt

Cinémathèque de Bretagne 4 rue Chalutier 'Le Forban', 22190 Plérin

Cinémathèque Universitaire Centre Censier, 13 rue Santeuil, 75005 Paris

Bibliothèque Nationale/Département de la Phonothèque et de l'Audiovisuel 2 rue Louvois, 75002 Paris

Établissement Cinématographique et Photographique des Armées (ECPA) Fort d'Ivry, 94205 Ivry, s/Seine Cedex

Stiftung Deutsche Kinemathek Pommernallee 1, 1000 Berlin 19

Münchner Stadtmuseum/Filmmuseum St Jakobs-Platz 1, 8000 Munich 2

Bundesarchiv-Filmarchiv Potsdamer Str. 1, D-5400 Koblenz (mailing address: Postfach 320, D-5400 Koblenz)

Deutsches Filmmuseum Schaumainkai 41, 6000 Frankfurt a.M. 70

Deutsches Institut für Filmkunde/Filmarchiv Kreuzberger Ring 56, D-65205, Wiesbaden (Documentation/Information: Schaumainkai 41, D-6000 Frankfurt a.M. 70)

National Film and Television Archive 21 Stephen Street, London W1P 1PL

Department of Film, Imperial War Museum Lambeth Road, London SE1 6HZ

Scottish Film Archive 74 Victoria Crescent Road, Glasgow G12 9JN

Wales Film and Television Archive Uned 1, Parc Gwyddoniaeth, Cefn Llan, Aberystwyth, Dyfed SY23 3AH

The Cinema Museum The Old Fire Station, 46 Renfrew Road, Kennington, London SE11 4NA

Tainiothiki tis Ellados Canari Street 1, 10671 Athens

Magyar Filmintezet/Filmarchivum Budakeszi ut 51/b, H-1021 Budapest

ICELAND
Kvikmyndasafn Islands Laugavegur 24, 101 Reykjavik (mailing address: PO Box 320, 121 Reykjavik)

INDIA
National Film Archive of India Law College Road, Poona 411 004

INDONESIA
Sinematek Indonesia 'Pusat Perfilman H. Usmar Ismail', Jl. Haji Rangkayo Rasuna Said, 12940 Jakarta

IRAN
Film-Khane-ye Melli-e Iran (National Film Archive of Iran) Ministry of Culture and Islamic Guidance, Baharestan Sq., 11365 Tehran (mailing address: PO Box 5158, 11365 Tehran)

IRELAND
The Irish Film Institute, Archive Section 6 Eustace Street, Dublin 2

ISRAEL
Archion Israeli Leseratim/Israel Film Archive/Jerusalem Cinémathèque Hebron Road, Jerusalem 91083 (mailing address: PO Box 8561, Jerusalem 91083)

Steven Spielberg Jewish Film Archive Box 65, Law Building, Hebrew University, Mt Scopus, Jerusalem 91905

ITALY
Cineteca del Comune di Bologna via Galliera 8, 40121 Bologna

Cineteca del Friuli via Osoppo 26, 33013 Gemona del Friuli (Udine)

Cineteca Italiana Villa Comunale, via Palestro 16, 20121 Milan

Cineteca Nazionale via Tuscolana 1524, 00173 Rome

Museo Nazionale del Cinema Palazzo Chiablese, Piazza San Giovanni 2, 10122 Turin

JAPAN
National Film Center/Archive 3–1–4 Takane, Sagamihara, Kanagawa-Ken 229

KOREA (DPR of)
Choson Minjujui Inmingonghwaguk Kugga Yonghwa Munhongo (National Film Archive of DPRK) 15 Sochangdong, Central District, Pyongyang

KOREA (REPUBLIC of)
Korean Film Archive 700 Seocho-dong, Seocho-gu, Seoul 137–070 (mailing address: Seocho PO Box 91, Seoul 137–600)

LUXEMBOURG
Cinémathèque Municipale de Luxembourg 10 rue Eugène Ruppert, L-2453, Luxembourg

MACEDONIA
Kinoteka na Makedonija Bul. Goce Delcev b.b., 91000 Skopje (mailing address: PO Box 161, 91000 Skopje)

Cineteca Nacional Av. México-Coyoacán 389, 03330 Mexico City, DF (mailing address: Col. Xoco, CP 03330 Mexico City, DF)

Filmoteca de la Unam San Ildefonso 43, 06020 Mexico City, DF (mailing address: Apartado Postal 45–002, 06020 Mexico City)

THE NETHERLANDS
Nederlands Filmmuseum Vondelpark 3, 1071 AA Amsterdam

Audiovisual Archive/Netherlands Government Information Service Noordeinde 64, The Hague (mailing address: Postbus 20006, 2500 EA The Hague)

NEW ZEALAND/AOTEAROA
The New Zealand Film Archive 82 Tory Street, Wellington (mailing address: PO Box 9544, Wellington)

NICARAGUA
Cinemateca Nacional de Nicaragua Apartado Postal 4642, Managua

NORWAY
Norsk Filminstitutt Grev Wedels plass 1–5, 0105 Oslo 1 (mailing adddress: Postboks 482 Sentrum, 0105 Oslo 1)

PERU
Filmoteca de Lima/Museo de Arte-Edubanco Paseo Colón 125, Lima 1

POLAND
Filmoteka Narodowa ul. Pulawska 61, 00975 Warsaw

PORTUGAL
Cinemateca Portuguesa Rua Barata Salgueiro 39, 1200 Lisbon

PUERTO RICO
Archivo de Imágenes en Movimiento/Archivo General de Puerto Rico Av. Ponce de Leon no. 500, Puerta de Tierra 00901 (mailing address: Apartado Postal 4184, San Juan de Puerto Rico)

RUMANIA
Arhiva Nationala de Filme Str. Julius Fucik 25, CNC pour ANF sect. 2, 7000 Bucharest (mailing address: Casuta Postala 126, Bucharest 1)

RUSSIA
Gosfilmofond of Russia Belye Stolby, Moskovskaia Oblast 142050

SLOVENIA
Arhiv Republike Slovenije Zvezdarska 1, 61001 Ljubljana

SPAIN
Arxiu d'Audiovisuals (Filmoteca) Generalitat de Catalunya Diputació 279, 08007 Barcelona

Filmoteca de la Generalitat Valenciana Plaça de l'Ajuntament 17, 46002 Valencia

Filmoteca Española Carretera Dehesa de la Villa, 28040 Madrid

Svenska Filminstitutet/Cinemateket Filmhuset, Borgvägen 1–5, S-102 52 Stockholm (mailing address: PB 27126, S-102 52 Stockholm)

Cinémathèque Suisse 3 Allée Ernest Ansermet, CH-1003 Lausanne (mailing address: Case postale 2512, CH-1002 Lausanne)

The National Film Archive 4 Chao Fa Road, 10200 Bangkok

Sinema–TV Enstitüsü 80700 Kişlaönü – Beşiktaş, Istanbul

UN Visual Materials Library/Information Products Division Department of Public Information, Room S-805-N, United Nations, New York, NY 10017

Academy Film Archive Center for Motion Picture Study, 333 S. La Cienega Boulevard, Beverly Hills, CA 90211

Anthology Film Archives 32 Second Avenue at Second Street, New York, NY 10003

George Eastman House – International Museum of Photography and Film 900 East Avenue, Rochester, NY 14607

Human Studies Film Archives National Museum of Natural History, Room E307.123, Smithsonian Institution, Washington, DC 20560

Library of Congress Motion Picture, Broadcasting and Recorded Sound Division Washington, DC 20540

Motion Picture, Sound and Video Branch, National Archives Washington, DC 20408

Museum of Jewish Heritage 342 Madison Avenue, Suite 717, New York, NY 10173

The Museum of Modern Art/Department of Film 11 West 53rd Streeet, New York, NY 10019

National Center for Film and Video Preservation at the American Film Institute (East Coast) The John F. Kennedy Center for the Performing Arts, Washington, DC 20566; (West Coast) 2021 North Western Avenue, Los Angeles, CA 90027 (mailing address: PO Box 27999, Los Angeles, CA 90027)

The National Center for Jewish Film Lown Building 102, Brandeis University, Waltham, MA 02254

Pacific Film Archive University Art Museum, 2625 Durant Avenue, Berkeley, CA 94720

UCLA Film and Television Archive University of California, Los Angeles, 1438 Melnitz Hall, 405 Hilgard Avenue, Los Angeles, CA 90024–1622

Wisconsin Center for Film and Theater Research 412 Historical Society, 816 State Street, Madison, WI 53706

Archivo Nacional de la Imagen – Sodre   C.C. 1412, Sarandi 430, 1° piso, 11.000 Montevideo

Cinemateca Uruguaya Lorenzo Carnelli 1311, 11200 Montevideo (mailing address: Castilla 1170, Montevideo)

Filmoteca Vaticana   Palazzo San Carlo, 00120 Vatican City

Audiovisual Archive/Biblioteca Nacional   Calle Soledad con Las Piedritas, Edif. Rogi, Zona industrial de La Trinidad, Caracas 1010 (mailing address: Apartado Postal 6525, Caracas 1010)

Vien Tu Lieu Phim Viet Nam (Vietnam Film Institute)   Ngoc Khahn Street 115, Hanoi

Jugoslovenska Kinoteka   Knez Mihajlova 19/I, 11000 Belgrade

National Archives of Zimbabwe/Audiovisual Archive   Private Bag 7729, Causeway, Harare

Appendix III

DATING PATHÉ FILMS BY THEIR EDGE MARKS

Boxes divided by a dotted line indicate that each edge of the film stock bears a different inscription. In positive prints from the 1921–1927 period, the inscription is followed by four digits: the first two correspond to the year.

1899– April 1905	[no writing along the edges]
April– December 1905	PATHE FRERES PARIS 1905
1906– April 1907	PATHE FRERES PARIS
May– December 1907	PATHE FRERES .... 14 RUE FAVART PARIS
1908	PATHE FRERES 14 RUE FAVART PARIS .... EXHIBITION INTERDITE EN FRANCE ET EN SUISSE
1909– 1911	PATHE FRERES 14 RUE FAVART PARIS .... EXHIBITION INTERDITE EN FRANCE EN SUISSE EN BELGIQUE [or ET EN BELGIQUE]
end 1911– 1912	PATHE FRERES 14 RUE FAVART PARIS .... EXHIBITION INTERDITE EN FRANCE EN SUISSE EN BELGIQUE ET EN ITALIE
end 1912– 1913	[the same, in lower-case italics]
1913	[the same, in lower-case print]

end 1913– 1914	[the same, in taller, narrower print]
1914	PATHE FRERES PARIS [in taller, narrower print] or [no inscription along the edges]
1921	PATHE CINEMA FRANCE or PATHE CINEMA PARIS 16.. or 17..
1922	[the same] 18.. or 19.., 20.., 21..
1923	[the same] 22.. or 23.., 24.., 25..
1924	[the same] 26.. or 27..
1925	[the same] 28..or 29..
1926	[the same] 30.. or 31..
1927	[the same] 32.. or 33.., 34.., 35.., 36..

Sources: Gerhard Lamprecht, Harold Brown

APPENDIX IV

EASTMAN KODAK EDGE CODES, 1913 – 1928

From 1916 onwards, the Eastman Kodak company manufactured most of the film stock in the silent period. Its only significant rivals were Agfa, Brifco, Gevaert and, for a while, Pathé. Eastman Kodak marked its film stock with date codes along the edges (see Plate 22). Today these codes are a great help in identifying prints. The symbols can be found between the perforations and the edge of the film, immediately after the word 'Kodak', which is repeated along the length of the print. The same procedure was used from 1917 for prints made in the United Kingdom, and from 1925 for prints made in Canada.

In 1927 Kodak absorbed the laboratories which produced Pathé film stock in France. From then on, Pathé film still bears the name of the original company along the edges of the print, but sometimes the Kodak date codes for the United Kingdom can also be found there.

Initially, when date codes were used on prints manufactured in the first six months of the year, the symbols were reproduced immediately after the word 'Kodak'; in the second half of the year, there was approximately one centimetre distance between them.

Beware: the codes indicate the year when the film stock was manufactured, which does not necessarily correspond to the year when the film was exposed or processed. A date code may be earlier than the year in which the corresponding film was shot.

Codes are printed on a film by means of a photographic process. They show up as black characters on a clear background on the stock on which they were printed originally. Obviously, these codes can be reproduced on a later print generation, where they will appear as clear characters on a black background. In the next print generation the codes become black marks on a clear background once again, as in the original, and so on from generation to generation. This must be borne in mind so that one does not become confused or make mistakes when codes from a certain year appear on a film which was made at a later date, or when several different codes are found on the same print.

These rules do not always hold true for 'reversal' film. There we find, in some cases, clear characters on black edges; elsewhere the codes are black on clear areas.

Kodak film made before the introduction of date codes can sometimes be dated as well: between 1913 and 1916, the stock is marked with the word 'Eastman'. The letters are stencilled in large capital letters from 1913 to the first half of 1914 (see Plate 40). From the second half of 1914 and throughout 1915, the letters become smaller and are preceded by a small rectangle placed two or three frames away. From the beginning of 1916 onwards, the rectangle is replaced by two black dots.

Year	United States (Rochester)	United Kingdom (Harrow)	Canada
1913–summer 1914	ʁ A S T M A ʌ (EASTMAN, stencilled)		
summer 1914–end 1915	▬ E A S T M A N		
early 1916	●● E A S T M A N		
1916	●		
1917	■	◡	
1918	▲	L	
1919	● ●	—	
1920	■ ■	◡ ◡	
1921	▲ ▲	L L	
1922	● ■	— —	
1923	● ▲	◡ L	
1924	▲ ■	— L	
1925	■ ●	◡ —	● L
1926	▲ ●	— ◡	● —
1927	■ ▲	L —	● ◡
1928	● ● ●	L ◡	L ●

Source: Harold Brown

107

APPENDIX V

BIBLIOGRAPHICAL REFERENCES

Chapter 1: What Is a Silent Film?

More details about the physical and the technical characteristics of silent films can be found in Eileen Bowser and John Kuiper (eds.), *A Handbook for Film Archives* (New York and London: Garland, 1991); in the multi-authored *Preservation and Restoration of Moving Images and Sound* (Brussels: FIAF, 1986); and in Raymond Fielding (ed.), *A Technological History of Motion Pictures and Television* (Berkeley and Los Angeles: University of California Press, 1967).

An outline of formats other than 35mm can be found in Glenn E. Matthews and Raife G. Tarkington, 'Early History of Amateur Motion-Picture Film', *Journal of the Society of Motion Picture and Television Engineers*, vol. 64, no. 3, March 1955, pp. 105–16; this outline can be completed by consulting Brian Coe, *The History of Movie Photography* (Westfield, NJ: Eastview, 1981), pp. 162–9.

The biannual *Bulletin FIAF*, the publication of the Fédération Internationale des Archives du Film (190 rue Franz Merjay, 1180 Brussels, Belgium), carries updates on the subject of film conservation and restoration techniques. The *Bulletin* has been retitled *Journal of Film Preservation* from issue 47, 1993. A full bibliography on this subject, updated to 1985, can be found in *Film da salvare: Guida alla conservazione e al restauro* (Milan: SugarCo, 1986, a special issue of *Comunicazione di massa*, vol. 5 no. 3, 1985). The British Film Institute distributes a training video, *The Work of a Film Archive* (Orly Yadin, Flashback Television Ltd, 1992, 27'13″, VHS PAL), providing an introductory overview of the range of technical issues involved in film preservation and restoration. An illuminating and controversial analysis of technical, political and financial aspects of film restoration policies in the United States is provided by Annette Melville and Scott Simmon in *Film Preservation 1993: A Study of the Current State of American Film Preservation*, 4 vols. (Washington DC: National Film Preservation Board of the Library of Congress, 1993).

Those who wish to delve deeper into the subject of colour should start with Brian Coe, 'The Development of Colour Cinematography', in Roger Manvell (ed.), *The International Encyclopedia of Film* (New York: Crown, [1972]), pp. 29–32, and, by the same author, 'The History of Movie Photography', ibid., pp. 112–39; next would be Jacques Marette, 'Les procédés de coloriage mécanique des films', *Bulletin de l'Association Française des Ingénieurs et Techniciens du Cinéma*, no. 7, 1950, pp. 3–8; Esperanza Londoño, *Pour une histoire de la couleur au cinéma*, graduate thesis, Université Sorbonne Nouvelle (DERCAV), Paris, 1985; Robert A. Nowotny, *The Way of All Flesh Tones: A History of Motion Picture Processes, 1895–1929* (New York and London: Garland, 1983).

Among the contemporary texts we must mention David S. Hulfish, *Cyclopedia of Motion-Picture Work* (Chicago: American Technical Society, 1918), vol. 1, pp. 262–77; vol. 2, pp. 149–54 (the reprint of an earlier 1915 edition, in a single volume, was published in New York by Arno Press/The New York Times under the title *Motion Picture Work*); *Le Film vierge Pathé* (Paris: Etablissements Pathé, 1926); *Tinting and Toning of Motion Picture Films* (Rochester: Eastman Kodak

Company, 1916), later updated in the 1918, 1922, 1924 and 1927 editions; M. Ruot and L. Didiée, 'The Pathé Kinematograph colour process', *The Photographic Journal*, vol. 45 (n.s., vol. 49), no. 3, March 1925, pp. 121–6; Frederick A. Talbot, *Moving Pictures: How They Are Made and Worked* (London: Heinemann, 1912), pp. 287–300.

An excellent summary of experiments with sound cinema during the first thirty years of the 20th century can be found in Brian Coe, 'The History of Movie Photography', pp. 90–111. Two very complete introductions to music in the silent cinema are by Gillian B. Anderson (ed.), *Music for Silent Films, 1894–1929: A Guide* (Washington DC: Library of Congress, 1988) and *Music for Silent Films: A Guide* (New York: Gordon Press, 1991); see also Hans-Jörg Pauli, *Filmmusik: Stummfilm* (Stuttgart: Klett-Cotta, 1981); Charles Hofmann, *Sounds for Silents* (New York: Drama Book Specialists, 1970); Charles M. Berg, *An Investigation of the Motives for and Realization of Music to Accompany the American Silent Film, 1896–1927* (New York: Arno Press, 1976); Walther Seidler (ed.), *Stummfilmmusik gestern und heute* (Berlin: Volker Spiess Verlag, 1979); Martin Marks, 'Film Music: The Material, Literature and Present State of Research', *The Quarterly Journal of the Music Library Association*, vol. 36 no. 2, 1979, pp. 282–325; David Robinson, *Musica delle ombre / Music of the Shadows* (suppl. to *Griffithiana*, vol. 13 nos. 38–39, October 1990); Sergio Miceli, *La Musica nel film: Arte e artigianato* (Fiesole: Discanto Edizioni, 1982).

A bibliography of more than 800 titles, mostly giving contemporary sources, can be found in Steven D. Wescott (ed.), *A Comprehensive Bibliography of Music for Film and Television*, Detroit Studies in Music Bibliography 54 (Detroit, Mich.: Information Coordinators, Inc, 1985), pp. 25–67). Those wishing to go further into the subject should look for the following original texts: Edith Lang and George West, *Musical Accompaniment of Moving Pictures* (Boston, Mass.: Boston Music, 1920; reprinted, New York: Arno Press, 1970); E. A. Ahern, *What and How to Play for Pictures* (Twinfalls, Idaho: Newsprint, 1913); John S. Zamecnik (ed.), *Sam Fox Moving Picture Music* (Cleveland: Sam Fox, 1913 [vols. 1 and 2], 1914 [vol. 3]); Giuseppe Becce, *Kinobibliothek* (Berlin: Schlesingersche Buch-und Musikhandlung Robert Lienau, 1919 ff.); George W. Beynon, *Musical Presentation of Motion Pictures* (New York: G. Schirmer, 1921); P. Kevin Buckley, *The Orchestral and Cinema Organist* (London: Hawkes, 1923); Erno Rapee, *Motion Picture Moods for Pianists and Organists: A Rapid-Reference Collection of Selected Pieces* (New York: G. Schirmer, 1924; reprinted, New York: Arno Press, 1970) and, by the same author, *Encyclopedia of Music for Pictures* (New York: Belwin, 1925; reprinted, New York: Arno Press, 1970); *Cinema Music as a Profession* (Torquay: Educational Section, Screen Music Society, 1925); Hans Erdmann and Giuseppe Becce, *Allgemeines Handbuch der Film-Musik I & II* (Berlin-Leipzig: Schlesingersche Buch- und Musikhandlung Robert Lienau, 1927). Jan Olsson's book *Från filmljud till ljudfilm* (Stockholm: Proprius Förlag, 1986) is accompanied by an audio cassette containing 17 recordings from phonograph records for silent films from the 1903–14 period.

The most reliable text on the problem of the projection speed of silent films is still the one by Kevin Brownlow, 'Silent Films: What Was the Right Speed?', *Sight and Sound*, Summer 1980, and *Classic Images*, June 1984. The question is examined in more depth by Richard Koszarski in *An Evening's Entertainment: The Age of the Silent Feature Picture, 1915–1929*, vol. 3 of the *History of the American Cinema*, Charles Harpole, general editor (New York: Scribner's, 1990), pp. 56–9; a heterodox point of view on this subject is set out by James Card in 'Silent-Film Speed', *Image*, vol. 4 no. 7, October 1955, reproduced in Marshall Deutelbaum (ed.), *'Image' on the Art and Evolution of Film* (New York and Rochester: Dover Publications Inc. and International Museum of Photography at George Eastman House, 1979), pp. 145–6.

Two classics on the architecture of auditoriums are David Atwell, *Cathedrals of the Movies: A History of British Cinemas and Their Audiences* (London : The Architectural Press, 1980) and Ben M. Hall, *The Best Remaining Seats* (New York: Bramhall House, 1961). To these we must add (especially for its precious final bibliography) Joseph M. Valerio and Daniel Friedman, *Movie Palaces: Renaissance and Reuse* (New York: Educational Facilities Laboratories Division, Academy for Educational Development, 1982).

In the absence of a general history of film reception during the silent period, we should treasure the lucid observations on the subject by Yuri Tsivian, *Historiceskaja recenija kino kinematograph v Rossii, 1896–1930* (Riga: Zinatne, 1991), translated into English as *Early Cinema in Russia and its Cultural Reception* (London: Routledge, 1994).

I am grateful to Riccardo Redi for his corrections and additions to this chapter.

Chapter 2: Where Are the Prints?

A fascinating introduction to the world of film archives is Raymond Borde's *Les Cinémathèques* (Paris: L'Age d'Homme, 1983), complemented by *50 ans d'archives du film* (Brussels: FIAF , 1988), which contains a brief description of the collections in the FIAF archives; the most recent publications are Penelope Houston's *Keepers of the Frame: The Film Archives* (London: British Film Institute, 1994); Anthony Slide, *Nitrate Won't Wait: A History of Film Preservation in the United States* (Jefferson, NC, and London: McFarland, 1992); David Francis, 'Definition et fonction des archives cinématographiques', in Emmanuelle Toulet (ed.), *Ciné-Mémoire* (Paris: Centre National de la Cinématographie / Ministére de la Culture et de la Communication, 1991), pp. 29–33. Two brief but illuminating accounts of the situation in Europe and in the United States can be found in the report edited in 1991 by Michelle Aubert on behalf of the Association des Cinémathéques de la Communauté Européenne, *Les archives et les cinémathèques européennes: état de leurs activités*, and in David Francis, 'Film Conservation Center. A Pioneer in Saving Movies', *Library of Congress Information Bulletin*, vol. 50 no. 1, 14 January 1991, pp. 3–6.

The comments in this chapter should have made it clear that the best way to obtain up-to-date information on material available for consultation is to ask the archives directly (the few lists which have been published go out of date very quickly). Despite the inevitable inaccuracies, due to the provisional nature of the cataloguing systems in many of the film archives that took part in the project, of fundamental importance is Ronald S. Magliozzi (ed.), *Treasures from the Film Archives: A Catalog of Short Silent Fiction Films Held by FIAF Archives* (Metuchen, NJ, and London: The Scarecrow Press, 1988), containing the titles of nine thousand silent 'shorts' preserved by various institutions belonging to FIAF.

The following catalogues are also very useful: *National Film Archive Catalogue of Viewing Copies: British Films* [provisional title] (London: British Film Institute, forthcoming in 1995); *National Film Archive Catalogue of Viewing Copies 1985* (ibid., 1984); *National Film Archive Catalogue: Part I, Silent News Films, 1895–1933* (ibid., 1965); *Part II, Silent Non-Fiction Films, 1895–1934* (ibid., 1960); *Part III, Silent Fiction Films (1895–1930)* (ibid., 1966); *National Film Archive Catalogue*, vol. 1: *Non-Fiction Films* (ibid., 1980); Jon Gartenberg (ed.), *The Film Catalog: A List of Holdings in the Museum of Modern Art* (Boston, Mass.: G. K. Hall & Co, 1985); *Circulating Film Library Catalog* (New York: The Museum of Modern Art, 1984); *Circulating Film and Video Catalog*, vol. 2 (New York: The Museum of Modern Art, 1990); Richard Prelinger and Celeste R. Hoffman (eds.), *Footage '89: North American Film and Video Sources* (New York: Prelinger, 1989) in conjunction with the updated volume *Footage '91* (New York: Prelinger, 1991). The Cinémathèque Française has published annual lists of the films they restored and printed: *Restaurations et tirages de la Cinémathèque Française* (vols. 1–4, 1986–89). Information on the surviving Russian and German silent films can be found in two vols. edited for the Pordenone Silent Film Festival: *Silent Witnesses: Russian Films, 1908–1919* (Pordenone: Edizioni Biblioteca dell'Immagine / London: British Film Institute, 1989; distributed in the United States by Indiana University Press) and *Before Caligari: German Cinema, 1895–1920* (Pordenone: Biblioteca dell'Immagine, 1990, distributed in the United States by the University of Wisconsin Press). On the legal aspects of obtaining access to prints, see Birgit Kofler, *Legal Questions Facing Audiovisual Archives* (Paris: UNESCO, 1991).

An important opportunity to look at films outside film archives – especially useful for those who cannot afford frequent travel – is provided by the annual silent film festival, the Giornate del Cinema Muto held in Pordenone. One can attend by writing to the Cineteca del Friuli, via Osoppo 26, 33013 Gemona del Friuli (Udine), Italy. Important retrospectives are organised at many FIAF archives and by festivals in Syracuse, NY (Cinefest), Los Angeles (Cinecon), Paris (Ciné-Mémoire), Bologna (Cinema Ritrovato), Pesaro (Mostra del Nuovo Cinema), as well as in the meetings of Domitor (c/o Département d'histoire de l'art/cinéma, Université de Montréal, CP 6128, Succursale A, Montréal, Québec H3C 3J7, Canada), an international association promoting research on early cinema.

Chapter 3: Research Material

The university student, the cinephile and the non-specialised spectator all face the same question: where does one begin reading to embark on the silent cinema adventure? A single definitive answer does not exist. Much depends on each person's tastes, ambitions and needs. However, there are several possible answers: some film historians have pointed to the titles they consider essential as the first phase of research into images of the past, or which formed and nourished their own burning passion for the silent cinema. These, therefore, are deliberately partial and personal suggestions. They can, however, help us to understand the historians' intellectual development and perhaps to retrace the path they followed.

Kevin Brownlow suggests Maurice Bardèche and Robert Brasillach, *Histoire du cinéma* (Paris: Denoël et Steele, 1935), 'The first I read'; George C. Pratt, *Spellbound in Darkness* (Greenwich, Conn.: New York Graphic Society, 1973); *Classics of the Silent Film* (New York: Bramhall House, 1959), signed by Joe Franklin but owed above all to William K. Everson; Lewis Jacobs, *The Rise of the American Film* (New York: Harcourt & Brace, 1939): 'What an incredible job for one so young!'; Walter Kerr, *The Silent Clowns* (reprinted 1989, New York: Da Capo Press); Richard Griffith and Arthur Mayer, *The Movies* (New York: Simon & Schuster, 1957); David Robinson, *Chaplin: His Life and Art* (London: Collins, 1985); William K. Everson, *The American Silent Film* (New York: Oxford University Press, 1978); Jay Leyda, *Kino. A History of Russian and Soviet Film* (London: George Allen & Unwin, 1960; third edition, Princeton, NJ: Princeton University Press, 1983); Karl Brown, *Adventures With D. W. Griffith* (New York: Farrar, Straus & Giroux, 1973); 'And I would urge [you] to go back to the fan magazines of the time' as well as to 'Marshall Deutelbaum (ed.), *'Image' on the Art and Evolution of the Film*, which I liked very much.' Most frequently consulted volumes: Dennis Gifford, *British Film Catalogue* (mentioned below in the filmography section); Raymond Chirat, *Catalogue des films français de long métrage: films de fiction, 1919–1929* (Toulouse: Cinémathèque de Toulouse, 1984); *The American Film Institute Catalog of Motion Pictures Produced in the United States*, vol. F1: *Feature Films, 1911–1920* (Berkeley: University of California Press, 1988); *The American Film Institute Catalog of Motion Pictures Produced in the United States*, vol. F2: *Feature Films, 1921–1930* (New York: R. R. Bowker, 1971).

Davide Turconi emphasises the continuing fundamental importance of the histories of the cinema by Georges Sadoul: *Histoire générale du cinéma*: vol. 1: 1832–97; vol. 2: 1897–1909; vol. 3: 1909–20 (Paris: Denoël, 1946–52) and by Jean Mitry: *Histoire du cinéma: art et industrie*: vol. 1: 1895–1914; vol. 2: 1915–25; vol. 3: 1923–30 (Paris: Editions Universitaires, 1967–73), 'The first for those who are able to correct its ideological tendencies, the second because it is based on an exceptional memory of films seen'. He suggests that they should be taken together with Jean Mitry's *Esthétique et psychologie du cinéma* (Paris: Presses Universitaires de France, 1963), Barry Salt's *Film Style & Technology: History & Analysis* (London: Starword, 1983; second edition, 1988) and Francesco Savio's *Visione Privata* (Rome: Bulzoni, 1972). Turconi also mentions some texts on the 'national film movements': Lewis Jacobs, *The Rise of the American Film* and Walter Kerr, *The Silent Clowns* for the United States; Aldo Bernardini, *Cinema muto italiano, 1896–1914* (Bari: Laterza, 1980–1982, 3 vols.) and Gian Piero Brunetta, *Storia del cinema italiano, 1895–1945*, 2nd edition, revised and enlarged (Rome: Editori Riuniti, 1993) for Italy; for Great Britain, Rachael Low, *The History of the British Film* (London: George Allen & Unwin, 1948 [vol. 1: 1896–1906, in collaboration with Roger Manvell], 1949 [vol. 2: 1906–1914], 1950 [vol. 3: 1914–1918], 1971 [vol. 4: 1918–1929]); Jay Leyda, *Kino. A History of Russian and Soviet Film*, integrated into *Silent Witnesses*, for Russia and the Soviet Union.

Roland Cosandey believes that the analysis of films should be accompanied, according to the linguistic or the national context in question, by a direct knowledge of the contemporary written sources (from production catalogues to critical and corporate magazines, without excluding the popular press and cinema programmes) and of some fundamental texts only partially available in anthologies: Richard Abel, *French Film Theory and Criticism: A History/Anthology, 1907–1939* (Princeton, NJ: Princeton University Press, 1988); Fritz Güttinger, *Kein Tag ohne Kino. Schriftsteller über den Stummfilm* (Frankfurt-am-Main: Deutsches Filmmuseum, 1984); Anton Kaes, *Kino-Debatte: Texte zum Verhältnis von Literatur und Film, 1909–1929* (Tübingen-Munich: Niemeyer-Deutscher Taschenbuch-Verlag, 1978); Alberto Abruzzese, *Introduzione allo studio delle teoriche cinematografiche americane, 1910–1929* (Venice: La Biennale di Venezia, 1975); George Pratt, *Spellbound in Darkness*. According to Cosandey, 'A solid bibliographic preparation, though made difficult by the fact that bibliographic materials are scattered and rare, is as indispensable as an innate distrust of memoirs in general. One should preferably consult texts in their original edition: critical editions are extremely rare and mainly deal with the work of film theoreticians.' These are some examples – limited to the period before 1916 – of publications essential to a general knowledge of the subject: Bolesław Matuszewski, *Une Nouvelle source de l'histoire* and *La Photogra-*

phie animée (Paris: Noizette, 1898), reprinted in Zbigniew Czeczot-Gawrak (ed.), *Bołeslaw Matus-zewski i jego pionierska mysl filmowa* (Warsaw: Filmoteka Polska, 1980); Georges Méliès, 'Les vues cinématographiques', in *Annuaire général et international de la photographie* (Paris: Plon, 1907); Eugène Babin, 'Les coulisses du cinématographe', 'Dans les coulisses du cinématographe', 'Le théâtre cinématographique', *L'Illustration* (Paris), 3396, 28 March 1908; 3397, 4 April 1908; 3427, 31 October 1908; Georg Cohn, *Kinematographenrecht* (Berlin: Decker's Verlag, 1909); Victorin Jasset, 'Etudes sur la mise en scène en cinématographie', *Ciné-Journal*, 165–168 and 170, October–November 1911; Emilie Altenloh, *Zur Soziologie des Kinos* (Jena: Verlag Eugen Diedrichs, 1913); Hugo Münsterberg, *The Photoplay: A Psychological Study* (New York: Appleton & Co, 1916).

Eileen Bowser includes in her list 'books by literate and intelligent people about their own experiences or who were close to the events': Linda Arvidson, *When the Movies Were Young* (New York: E. P. Dutton & Company, 1925); Fred Balshofer and Arthur C. Miller, *One Reel a Week* (Berkeley and Los Angeles: University of California Press, 1967); Karl Brown, *Adventures with D. W. Griffith*; Edward Wagenknecht, *The Movies in the Age of Innocence* (Norman, Okla.: University of Oklahoma Press, 1962); King Vidor, *A Tree Is a Tree* (New York: Harcourt, Brace, 1952); and 'for its testimony from the period as well as informed commentary', George Pratt, *Spellbound in Darkness*; 'for a good survey of the social forces in the period', Lary May, *Screening Out the Past: The Birth of Mass Culture and the Motion Picture Industry* (New York and Oxford: Oxford University Press, 1980); 'for fresh source of material about the beginnings of cinema and some provocative ideas about it', Eric Barnouw, *The Magician and the Cinema* (New York: Oxford University Press, 1981); 'for a modern scholarly approach to the early days of cinema', Roger Holman and André Gaudreault (eds.), *Cinema 1900–1906: An Analytical Study* (Brussels: FIAF, 1982); Donald Crafton, *Before Mickey: The Animated Film, 1898–1928* (Cambridge, Mass., and London: The MIT Press, 1982); Tom Gunning, *David W. Griffith and the Origins of American Narrative Film* (Chicago: University of Illinois Press, 1991); Charles Musser, *The Emergence of Cinema: The American Screen to 1907* (New York: Scribner's, 1990); and 'I would add all the volumes of Sadoul's *Histoire du cinéma*; 'for my home library, all the reference sources', for example, *The American Film Institute Catalog, 1911–1920* and *1921–1930*, the *Catalog of Copyright Entries: Motion Pictures*, vol. 1: *1894–1912*; vol. 2: 1912–1939 (Washington DC: Library of Congress, Copyright Office, 1951–53; the first volume is now available from the US Department of Commerce, National Technical Information Service, Springfield, Va. 22161), Elias Savada, *The American Film Institute Catalog of Motion Pictures Produced in the United States: Film Beginnings, 1893–1910* (Los Angeles: The National Center for Film and Video Preservation, 1993, 4 vols.), Einar Lauritzen and Gunnar Lundquist, *American Film Index, 1908–1915: Motion Pictures, July 1908–December 1915* (Stockholm, Film Index, 1976; distributed by Akademibokhandeln, Stockholm Universitet), Einar Lauritzen and Gunnar Lundquist, *American Film Index, 1916–1920: Motion Pictures, January 1916–December 1920* (Stockholm: Film Index, 1984; distributed by Akademibok-handeln, Stockholm Universitet), the *WPA Film Index* (New York: The Museum of Modern Art Film Library/The H. W. Wilson Company, 1941 [vol. 1]; White Plains, NY: Kraus, 1985 [vols. 2 and 3]); 'and I would throw everything else out if I could have the complete run of the *Moving Picture World*'.

Kristin Thompson shares the preference for the volumes edited by the American Film Institute; the other most frequently consulted authors are Anna Brady (ed.), *Union List of Film Periodicals: Holdings of Selected American Collections* (Westport, Conn.: Greenwood Press, 1984); Richard Abel, *French Film Theory and Criticism, 1907–1939*; Robert C. Allen, *Vaudeville and Film, 1895–1915: A Study in Media Interaction* (New York: Arno Press, 1980); Donald Crafton, *Before Mickey*; Kristin Thompson, *Exporting Entertainment: America in the World Film Market, 1907–1934* (London: British Film Institute, 1985); David Bordwell, Janet Staiger and Kristin Thompson, *The Classical Hollywood Cinema: Film Style and Mode of Production to 1960* (London: Routledge & Kegan Paul, 1985); Hans Schleugl and Ernst Schmidt Jr., *Eine Subgeschichte des Films: Lexicon des Avant-garde-, Experimental- und Undergroundfilms* (Frankfurt-am-Main: Suhrkamp, 1974, 2 vols.); Gerhard Lamprecht, *Deutsche Stummfilme, 1903–1931* (Berlin: Stiftung Deutsche Kinemathek, 1967–70, 10 vols.); Raymond Chirat, *Catalogue des films français de long métrage: films de fiction, 1919–1929*; Kevin Brownlow, *The Parade's Gone By* (New York: Alfred A. Knopf, 1969).

Richard Koszarski offers a selection which coincides in part with some of the earlier ones: George Pratt, *Spellbound in Darkness*; William K. Everson, *The American Silent Film*; David

Bordwell, Janet Staiger and Kristin Thompson, *The Classical Hollywood Cinema*; John B. Rathbun, *Motion Picture Making and Exhibiting* (Los Angeles: Holmes, 1914); Terry Ramsaye, *A Million and One Nights* (New York: Simon & Schuster, 1926); Austin Lescarboura, *Behind the Motion Picture Screen* (New York: Munn, 1919); Homer Croy, *How Motion Pictures Are Made* (New York: Harper, 1918); Benjamin B. Hampton, *A History of the Movies* (New York: Covici, Friede, 1931). Among the 'indispensable' books, Koszarski also lists *A History of American Cinema* (New York: Scribner's, 1990), mentioned below in the list of works on the 'national movements', and three titles by Kevin Brownlow: *The Parade's Gone By*; *The War, the West, and the Wilderness* (New York: Knopf, 1979) and *Behind the Mask of Innocence* (New York: Knopf, 1991).

Other Reference Works

This bibliographical note does not aim to list the 'most important' books on the history of the cinema. However, some other reference works should always be kept at hand to refresh one's memory or to check a 'classic' author's point of view. As well as the often cited volumes by Sadoul and Mitry, one must know Jacques Deslandes and Jacques Richard, *Histoire comparée du cinéma*, vol. 1: *1826–1896*; vol. 2: *1897–1906* (Paris: Casterman, 1966–68) and Jerzy Toeplitz, *Historia sztuki filmowej* (Warsaw: Filmowa Agencja Wydawnicza, 1955; German trans.: *Geschichte des Films*, Munich: Rogner & Bernhard, 1973).

Concerning the pre-cinema period, the essential reference tool is Hermann Hecht's work, edited by Ann Hecht, *Pre-Cinema History: An Encyclopaedia and Annotated Bibliography of The Moving Image before 1896* (London: Bowker/Saur in association with The British Film Institute, 1993). A reading programme on the origins of the cinema in general should include Franz Paul Liesegang, *Moving and Projected Images: A Chronology of Pre-Cinema History* (London: The Magic Lantern Society of Great Britain, 1986); David Robinson, 'Masterpieces of animation, 1833–1908', special issue of *Griffithiana*, vol. 14, 43, December 1991; David Robinson also prepared *Origins of Cinema: Catalogue of an Exhibition Presented by Cumberland Row Antiques Ltd, July–August 1964* (London, 1964); Emmanuelle Toulet, *Cinématographe, invention du siècle* (Paris: Gallimard/Réunion des Musées Nationaux, 1988); *Cinema 1900–1906: An Analytical Study*; John L. Fell, *Film Before Griffith* (Berkeley: University of California Press, 1983); Paul C. Spehr, *The Movies Begin: Making Movies in New Jersey, 1887–1920* (Newark, NJ: The Newark Museum/Morgan & Morgan, 1977). Emmanuelle Toulet edited a *Bibliographie internationale du cinéma des premiers temps: Travaux des membres de Domitor* (Quebec: Domitor, 1987), providing a survey of international research on film production up to 1915. An amazing bibliography of cinema books published during the early period is the *Union Catalogue of Books and Periodicals Published Before 1914 Held by the Film Archives Members of the International Federation of Film Archives* (Brussels: FIAF, 1967), listing 914 titles held in the collections of the 24 archives which took part in the project.

An excellent starting point for studying silent cinema in the United States is provided by the first three volumes of *A History of the American Cinema*: vol. 1: Charles Musser, *The Emergence of Cinema: The American Screen to 1907*; vol. 2: Eileen Bowser, *The Transformation of Cinema: 1908–1915*; vol. 3: Richard Koszarski, *An Evening's Entertainment: The Age of the Silent Feature Picture, 1915–1928* (New York: Scribner's, 1990). For Britain, in addition to the works by Rachael Low cited by Turconi, see the texts by John Barnes, *The Beginnings of Cinema* in England (London: David & Charles, 1976), *The Rise of Cinema in Great Britain* (London: Bishopsgate Press, 1983), *Pioneers of the British Film* (London: Bishopsgate Press, 1983 [actually 1988]) and *Filming the Boer War* (London: Bishopsgate Press, 1991); a fifth volume is in preparation. Finally, for France, two books by Richard Abel are recommended: *The Ciné Goes to Town: French Cinema, 1896–1914* (Berkeley: University of California Press, 1994) and *French Cinema: The First Wave, 1915–1929* (Princeton, NJ: Princeton University Press, 1984).

Other Media

We must also mention the films and television programmes devoted to the silent cinema in general and to some of its most important personalities. A useful filmography has been compiled by Anthony Slide in *Films on Film History* (Metuchen, NJ, and London: Scarecrow Press, 1979); among more recent works, see Noël Burch, *Correction, Please; or, How We Got Into Pictures* (Arts Council of Great Britain, 16mm, 52', 1979); the television documentaries by Kevin Brownlow and David Gill, *Hollywood: The Pioneers* (Thames TV, 1980, 13 episodes of 52'30"; all sections were cut for American syndication, then restored to their complete length for PBS, laserdisc and video release), *Unknown Chaplin* (Thames TV, 1983, 3 episodes of 52'30"), *Buster Keaton: A Hard Act to Follow* (Thames TV, 1987, 3 episodes of 52'30"; episode 3 has been broadcast by Channel Four only in the United Kingdom); *Harold Lloyd, the Third Genius* (Thames TV, 1990, 2 episodes of 51'30"), and *D. W. Griffith, Father of Film* (Photoplay Productions, UK version: 3 episodes, 156'; US version: 6 parts, 165'; international version: 6 parts, 157'); Charles Musser, *Before the Nickelodeon: The Early Cinema of Edwin S. Porter* (Film for Thought/New Hollywood Feature Film, 1982, 16mm, 60'); Werner Nekes, *Was geschah wirklich zwischen den Bildern?* (Werner Nekes Filmproduktion, 1985, 16mm, 83', distributed in the United States by Kino International under the title *Film Before Film*).

As the origins of cinema overlap from a chronological point of view with those of television, it is useful to know at least the main stages of the technological development of the electronic image during the 'silent period'. A good introductory work is by Albert Abramson, *The History of Television, 1880 to 1941* (Jefferson, NC, and London: McFarland, 1987).

Filmographies

Filmographies are the blessing and the curse of those who study the silent cinema. None of them is perfect but one cannot do without them (a stimulating discussion of these problems is put forward by Geoffrey Nowell-Smith, 'Filmography', *Screen*, vol. 32 no. 4, Winter 1991, pp. 452–5). What follows is a partial list, arranged by country; those wishing for a fuller list may consult the volume by Dorothea Gebauer (edited by Harriet Harrison), *Bibliography of National Filmographies* (Brussels: FIAF, 1985).

Argentina: *La Epoca Muda del Cine Argentino*, 2nd edn. (Buenos Aires: Centro de Envestigación de la Historia del Cine Argentino, 1958 [second edition]).

Australia: Andrew Pike and Ross Cooper, *Australian Film, 1900–1977: A Guide to Feature Film Production* (Melbourne: Oxford University Press/The Australian Film Institute, 1980).

Austria: Walter Fritz, *Die Österreichischen Spielfilme der Stummfilmzeit (1907–1930)* (Vienna: Österreichisches Filmarchiv/Österreichische Gesellschaft für Filmwissenschaft, 1967).

Belgium: *Films Belges: documentaires, films de fiction, dessins animés, films d'archives, reportages* (Brussels: Quatre Bras 2, Ministère des Affaires Étrangères, du Commerce Extérieur et de la Coopération au Développement, 1974–75).

Brazil: Jean-Claude Bernardet, *Filmografia do Cinema Brasileiro: 1900–1935* (São Paulo: Secretaria da Cultura de São Paulo, 1979).

Bulgaria: Peter Kardzhilov, *Bulgarian Feature Films: An Annotated Illustrated Filmography*, vol. 1: *1915–1948*, (Sofia: Bulgarska Nacionalna Filmoteka, Dr Peter Beron State Publishing House, 1987).

Canada: D. J. Turner, *Canadian Feature Film Index/Index des films canadiens de long métrage, 1913–1985* (Ottawa: National Film, Television and Sound Archives/Archives nationales du film, de la télévision et de l'enregistrement sonore, 1987); Peter Morris (ed.), *Canadian Feature Films, 1913–1969*, Part 1: *1913–1940* (Ottawa: Canadian Film Institute, 1970).

China: Sergei Arkadevich Toroptsev, *Ocherk Istorii Kitaiskogo Kino, 1896–1966* (Moscow: Nauka, 1979); Jay Leyda, *Dianying: Electric Shadows. An Account of Films and the Film Audience in China* (Cambridge, Mass./London: MIT Press, 1972).

Czechoslovakia: Dr Jan S. Kolar and Myrtil Frida, *Československý Nemý Film 1898–1930* (Prague: Československý Film, 1957).

Denmark: Marguerite Engberg, *Registrant over danske film*, 1896–1930, vol. 1: *1896–1909*; vol. 2: *1910–1912* ; vol. 3: *1913–1914*; vol. 4: *1915–1917*; vol. 5: *1918–1930* (Copenhagen: Institut for Filmvidenskab, 1977–1982).

Finland: *Filmografia Fennica, 1904–1963* (Helsinki: Otava, 1965).

France: Raymond Chirat, *Catalogue des films français, 1919–1929* (a volume on the 1907–18 period, co-edited by Chirat and Eric Le Roy is in preparation); Henri Bousquet and Riccardo Redi (eds.), *Pathé Frères, 1896–1914*, Part 1 (1896–1906) (*Quaderni di Cinema*, vol. 8 no. 37, January–March 1988 [published in 1992]) ; Henri Bousquet, *Catalogue Pathé, 1907–1909* (Bures-sur-Yvette: Editions Henri Bousquet, 1993); further volumes on Pathé are in preparation; André Gaudreault edited the filmographic analysis of *Pathé 1900* (Ste Foy, Québec & Paris: Les Presses de l'Université Laval / Presses de la Sorbonne Nouvelle, 1993); *Gaumont: 90 ans de cinéma* (Paris: Ramsay/La Cinémathèque Française, 1986); Donald Crafton, *Emile Cohl, Caricature, and Film* (Princeton, NJ: Princeton University Press, 1990, pp. 341–75); Juan Gabriel Tharrats, *Los 500 films de Segundo de Chomón* (Saragossa: Prensas Universitarias, 1988) and *Inolvidable Chomón* (Murcia: Filmoteca Regional de Murcia, 1990); Madeleine Malthête-Méliès, Anne-Marie Quévrain and Jacques Malthête, *Essai de reconstitution du catalogue français de la Star-Film* (Bois d'Arcy : Centre National de la Cinématographie, 1981; a new updated version is forthcoming); Georges Sadoul, *Lumière et Méliès* (Paris: Lherminier, 1985: edition revised by Bernard Eisenschitz); Youen Bernard, *L'Eclipse*, graduate thesis (Paris: Université de Paris VIII, 1993); 'Société Française des Films et Cinématographes Eclair (1907–1919): A Checklist', *Griffithiana*, vol. 15 nos. 44 -45, May–September 1992, pp. 28–88.

Germany: Gerhard Lamprecht, *Deutsche Stummfilme*, and the labyrinthine Herbert Birett, *Das Filmangebot in Deutschland, 1895–1911* (Munich Filmbuchverlag Winterberg, 1991) and *Verzeichnis in Deutschland gelaufener Filme: Entscheidungen der Filmzensur, 1911–1920: Berlin, Hamburg, München, Stuttgart* (Munich: K. G. Saur, 1980), which deal with German and foreign films distributed in Germany.

Great Britain: Denis Gifford, *The British Film Catalogue, 1895–1985: A Reference Guide* (New York: Facts on File Publications, 1987) and the same author's *British Animated Films, 1895–1985: A Filmography* (Jefferson, NC: McFarland & Co., 1987).

Hungary: Ferenc Kovács (ed.), *Magyar Filmográfia, 1901–1961* (Budapest: Magyar Filmtudományi Intézet és Filmarchivum, 1963).

India: Firoze Rangoonwalla, *Indian Filmography: Silent and Hindi Films, 1897–1969* (Bombay: J. Udeshi, 1970); Ashish Rajadhyaksha and Paul Willemen, *Encyclopaedia of Indian Cinema* (London and New Delhi: British Film Institute/Oxford University Press, 1994).

Italy: *Elenco delle Pellicole Cinematografiche approvate dal Ministero dell'Interno, 1913–1925* (one copy is held in the Davide Turconi Archives, Amministrazione Provinciale di Pavia, Ufficio Cultura, Piazza Italia 2, 27100 Pavia); Aldo Bernardini (ed.), *Archivio del cinema italiano*, vol. 1: *Il cinema muto, 1905–1931* (Rome: Edizioni Anica, 1991); Vittorio Martinelli, *Il cinema muto italiano* (*Bianco & Nero*, vol. 53 nos. 1–2 and 3–4, 1992 [1914]; vol. 52 nos. 1–2 and 3–4, 1991 [1915]; vol. 51 nos. 1–2 and 3–4, 1990 [1916]; vol. 50 nos. 3–4, 1989 [1917]; vol. 50 nos. 1–2, 1989 [1918]; vol. 49 nos. 1–3, 1980 [1919]; vol. 49 nos. 4–6, 1980 [1920]; vol. 48 nos. 1–3, 1981 [1921–1922]; vol. 48 nos. 4–6, 1981 [1923–1931]; other volumes are in preparation); Carla Manenti, Nicolas Monti, Giorgio Nicodemi (eds.), *Luca Comerio fotografo e cineasta* (Milan: Electa Editrice, 1979, pp. 104–6); Aldo Bernardini and Vittorio Martinelli, *Roberto Roberti, direttore artistico* (Pordenone: Giornate del Cinema Muto, 1985); Vittorio Martinelli and Sergio Grmek Germani, *Il cinema di Augusto Genina* (Pordenone: Edizioni Biblioteca dell'Immagine, 1989); 'I film dell'Itala', in Paolo Cherchi Usai (ed.), *Giovanni Pastrone: Gli anni d'oro del cinema a Torino* (Turin : UTET, 1986, pp. 123–42); Aldo Bernardini (ed. in collaboration with Vittorio Martinelli), 'I comici del muto italiano', *Griffithiana*, vol. 8 nos. 24–25, October 1985, pp. 63– 134; Aldo Bernardini (ed.), 'I comici del muto italiano:

Aggiunte e correzioni', *Griffithiana*, vol. 9 nos. 26–27, September 1986, pp. 99–101. Vittorio Martinelli and Mario Quargnolo, *Maciste & Co., i giganti buoni del muto italiano* (Gemona del Friuli: Edizioni Cinepopolare, 1981); Aldo Bernardini and Vittorio Martinelli (eds.), *Francesca Bertini, 1892–1985* (Rome: Centro Sperimentale di Cinematografia, Cineteca Nazionale, 1985); Riccardo Redi, *La Cines: storia di una casa di produzione italiana* (Rome: CNC Edizioni, 1991), pp. 139–76. The *Storia del cinema muto italiano*, vol. 1, by Maria Adriana Prolo (Milan: Società Editrice Poligono, 1951, pp. 117–84), for many years the only source of general filmographic information on this subject, includes an approximate 'Elenco delle pellicole mute realizzate in Italia dal 1904 al 1915'.

Mexico: Federico Dávalos Orozco and Esperanza Vázquez Bernal, *Filmografia general del Cine Mexicano (1906–1931)* (Puebla: Universidad Autónoma de Puebla, 1985); Aurelio de Los Reyes, *Filmografia del Cine Mudo Mexicano 1896–1920* (Mexico City: Filmoteca Unam, 1986).

Netherlands: Karel Dibbets and Frank van der Maden (eds.), *Geschiedenis van de Nederlandse Film en Bioscoop tot 1940* (Weesp: Het Wereldvenster, 1986).

Norway: Leif-Erik Bech (ed.), *Norsk Filmografi, 1908–1979* (Oslo: Norsk kino-og Filmfond/ Norsk Filminstitutt, 1980); Øivind Hanche (ed.), *Register over Norske Langfilmer 1908–1.4.1990* (Oslo: Norsk Filminstitutt, 1990).

Poland: Jadwiga Bochenska and others (compiled by Jerzy Toeplitz), *Historia Filmu Polskiego*, vol. 1: *1895–1921* [with a filmography of silent fiction films produced between 1911 and 1929] (Warsaw: Wydawnicza Artystyczne i Filmowe, 1966).

Portugal: José de Matos-Cruz, *Prontuário do cinema portugues, 1896–1989* (Lisbon: Cinemateca Portuguesa, 1989).

Rumania: *Productia Cinematografică din România, 1897–1970; Filmografie Adnotată*, vol. 1 : *Cinematograful Mut* (1897–1930); vol. 2: *Filmul de Ficţiune* (Bucharest: Arhiva Nationala de Filme, 1970).

Russia: and the **Soviet Union**: Veniamin Vishnevskij, *Sovetskie Hudožestvennye fil'my. Annotirovannyj katalog*, vol. 1: *Nemye fil'my, 1918–1935* (Moscow: Iskusstvo, 1961); *Hudozestvennye fil'my dorevoljucionnoj Rossii: Fil'mograficeskoe opisanie: fil'my do 1917 goda* (Moscow: Goskinoizdat, 1945); A. A. Chernyshev, *Russkaia dooktiabr'skaia kinozhurnalistika* (Moscow: Moskovskogo Universiteta, 1987).

Spain: Palmira González Lopez and Joaquín T. Cánovas Belchi, *Catálogo del cine español*, vol. F2: *Peliculas de ficción (1921–1930)* (Madrid: Filmoteca Española, 1993).

Sweden: *Svensk filmografi* (Stockholm: Svenska Filminstitutet, 1986 [vol. 1: 1897–1919], 1982 [vol. 2: 1920–29], 1979 [vol. 3: 1930–39]).

Turkey: Agah Özgüc (ed.), *Türk Filimleri Sözlügü, 1914–1972* (Istanbul: Cahit Poyraz, 1963).

The United States: (in addition to the filmographies listed above by Eileen Bowser): Kemp R. Niver, *Motion Pictures from the Library of Congress Paper Print Collection, 1894–1912* (Berkeley: University of California Press, 1967); Cooper Graham and others (ed.), *David W. Griffith and the Biograph Company* (Metuchen, NJ, and London: The Scarecrow Press, 1985); Anthony Slide, *The Big V: A History of the Vitagraph Company*, rev. ed. (Metuchen, NJ, and London: The Scarecrow Press, 1987); Davide Turconi, 'Filmografia: La produzione Vitagraph dal 1905 al 1916', in Paolo Cherchi Usai (ed.), *Vitagraph Company of America. Il cinema prima di Hollywood* (Pordenone: Studio Tesi, 1987), pp. 443–634, plus a page of addenda (an American edition is in preparation by the Smithsonian Institution Press); Bebe Bergsten (ed.), *Biograph Bulletins, 1896–1908* (Los Angeles: Locare Research Group, 1971); *Biograph Bulletins, 1908–1912* (New York: Octagon Books, n. d. [1973]); Kalton C. Lahue, *Continued Next Week: A History of the Moving Picture Serial* (Norman,

Okla.: University of Oklahoma Press, 1964); Reese V. Jenkins (ed.), *Thomas A. Edison Papers* (Frederick, Md.: University Publications of America, 1985 [6 reels of 35mm microfilm, plus a 50-page guide]); Rita Horwitz and Harriet Harrison (eds.), *The George Kleine Collection of Early Motion Pictures in the Library of Congress: A Catalog* (Washington, DC: Library of Congress, 1980); Steven Higgins, 'I film di Thomas H. Ince', *Griffithiana*, vol. 7 nos. 18–21, October 1984, pp. 155–203, and 'American Eclair, 1911–1915: A filmographic chronology derived from the pages of *The Eclair Bulletin* and the trade press of the day', *Griffithiana*, vol. 15 nos. 44–45, May–September 1992, pp. 89–129; Brian Anthony and Andy Edmonds, 'Charley Chase: Filmography' in *Griffithiana*, vol. 16 nos. 48–49, October 1993, pp. 34–53; Davide Turconi, 'Filmografia di Larry Semon', *Cinegrafie*, vol. 1 no. 2, 1989, pp. 35–70, plus a page of addenda, and *Monty Banks: Biofilmografia* (Cesena: Quaderni del Centro Cinema, 1987); 'The Silent Films of Frank Borzage', *Griffithiana*, vol. 15 no. 46, December 1992, pp. 44–58; and the filmography of Raymond Griffith in 'Another Griffith', *Griffithiana*, vol. 14 nos. 40–42, October 1991, pp. 22–46; Robert Farr, 'Lloyd Hamilton Filmography', *Griffithiana*, vol. 15 nos. 44–45, May–September 1992, pp. 217–230; Denis Gifford, *American Animated Films: The Silent Era, 1897–1929* (Jefferson, NC, and London: McFarland, 1990); Russell Mervitt and J. B. Kaufman, 'Walt Disney Silent Filmography (1921–1928)', in *Nel paese delle meraviglie / Walt in Wonderland. The Silent Films of Walt Disney* (Pordenone: Le Giornate del Cinema Muto/Edizioni Biblioteca dell'Immagine, 1992), pp. 174–230. A filmography of the Thanhouser company (ed. by Q. David Bowers) is in preparation by the Library of Congress and the Smithsonian Institution Press.

Venezuela: Ricardo Tirado, *Memoria y notas del cine venezolano 1897–1959* (n. p.[Caracas]: Fundación Neumann, n. d.).

Contemporary Magazines

A listing of some magazines from the silent film period frequently used in the study of silent cinema includes: **Denmark**: *Filmen* (1911–18); **France**: *Phono-ciné-gazette* (1905–09), *Ciné-Journal* (1908–37), *Le Courrier cinématographique* (1911–14; 1917–36), *Ciné pour tous*, which later became *Cinéa-Ciné pour tous* and finally *Cinéa-Ciné pour tous réunis* (1919–32), *Le Cinéopse* (1919–67); **Germany**: *Lichtbild-Bühne* (1908–39), *Der Kinematograph* (1907–35), *Filmkurier* (1919–44), *Der Film* (1916–43), *Erste Internationale Filmzeitung* (1907–20); **Great Britain**: *The Bioscope* (1908?–32); *The Era*, 'British variety artists' trade paper, [containing] the most information on films in the period when music halls were the main screening venues' (letter from Ben Brewster to the author, 26 February 1992); *The Optical Magic Lantern Journal* (1899), which became *The Optical Lantern and Kinematograph Journal* (1904), was later renamed *The Kinematograph and Lantern Weekly* (1907) and finally became *The Kinematograph Weekly* (1919–60); **Italy**: *La vita cinematografica* (1910–34), *La Cine-Fono* (1908–27), *Lux* (1908–11?), *L'illustrazione cinematografica* (1912–16?), *La Rivista Cinematografica* (1920–42). A list of film periodicals published in Italy was compiled by Davide Turconi and Camillo Bassotto, *Il cinema nelle riviste italiane dalle origini ad oggi* (Venice: Edizioni Mostracinema, n. d. [1972]; a revised and updated edition, edited by Riccardo Redi is *Cinema scritto: Il catalogo delle riviste italiane del cinema, 1907–1944* (Rome: Associazione Italiana per le Ricerche di Storia del Cinema, 1992); **Russia**: *Kinoteatr i zhizn'* (1913), *Kinezhurnal* (1910–17), *Sine-fono* (1907–18), *Vestnik kinematografii* (1910–17); **Soviet Union**: *Kinofot* (1922), *Sovetskij ekran* (1925–29); **Sweden**: *Filmbladet* (1915–ca. 1925); **United States**: *The Moving Picture World* (1907–27), *The New York Dramatic Mirror* (1879–1922), *Motography, Moving Picture News* (1908–13), *Motion Picture News* (1913–30), *The New York Clipper*. Two vast collections of reviews from the period have been published in facsimile editions: *Variety Film Reviews*: vol. 1: 1907–20; vol. 2, 1921–25; vol. 3: 1926–29; vol. 16: Index to Titles (New York: Garland Press, 1983), and *The New York Times Film Reviews, 1913–1968* (New York: The New York Times/Arno Press, 1970).

Modern Magazines

The contemporary magazines which most frequently address the silent cinema include: *Archives* (Institut Jean Vigo, 21 rue Mailly, 66000 Perpignan); *Cinémathèque* (c/o Cinémathèque Française, 29 rue du Colisée, 75008 Paris); *Film History* (1987–1990); new series (1993–sqq, London: John Libbey, 13 Smiths Yard, Summerley Street, London SW18 4HR); *Griffithiana* (Cineteca del Friuli, via Osoppo 26, 33013 Gemona del Friuli [Udine]); *Immagine* (Associazione Italiana per le Ricerche di Storia del Cinema, via Villafranca 20, 00185 Rome); *KINtop* (1992–sqq, Stroemfeld / Roter Stern, Oetlingerstrasse 19, CH-4007, Basle, and Holzhausenstrasse 4, D-6000 Frankfurt-am-Main); *1895* (Association Française de Recherche sur l'Histoire du Cinéma, c/o Jean A. Gili, 15 rue Lakanal, 75015 Paris); *Bulletin Domitor* (Département d'histoire de l'art/cinéma, Université de Montréal, CP 6128, Succursale A, Montréal, Québec H3C 3J7). An annually update list of articles on the silent cinema can be obtained from the following sources: Michael Moulds, *International Index to Film Periodicals* (New York: R. R. Bowker, 1972–1973; London: St James Press, 1974–1978; Brussels: FIAF, 1979–sqq; also available on CD-rom); Kevin Jack Hagopian, *Film Literature Index* (Albany, NY: State University of New York at Albany, 1973–sqq).

Chapter 4: Viewing Practice

There is virtually no literature on this subject. A general outline of the problems of access to film collections can be found in *Documents that Move and Speak: Audiovisual Archives in the New Information Age* (Munich: K. G. Saur, 1992). A guide to archival terminology is Günter Schulz and Hans Karnstädt, *Terms and Methods for Technical Archiving of Audiovisual Materials* (Munich-New York-Paris: K. G. Saur, 1992). The problem of identifying early films has been treated by Harold Brown in *Physical Characteristics of Early Films as Aids to Identification* (Brussels: FIAF, 1990) and by Suzanne Richard in 'Pathé, marchio di fabbrica', *Segnocinema*, vol. 6 no. 23, 1986, pp. 74–7 (a revised, French version of the essay was published in *1895*, no. 10, 1991, pp. 13–25).

Ethical problems concerning research in film archives are confronted in Paolo Cherchi Usai, 'Archive of Babel', *Sight and Sound*, vol. 59 no. 1, 1990, pp. 48– 50. The Fédération Internationale des Archives du Film is preparing two manuals: one outlining film projection standards, by Jean-Pierre Verscheure, and one for conducting scholarly research in 'film study centres', an organisational model which exists or is being developed in various institutions.

Chapter 5: Silent Cinema Revisited

Recently, debates about film restoration criteria have become increasingly lively, even though the participants are not always sufficiently aware of the philosophical issues involved. A well thought-out and effective summary of the present situation is Eileen Bowser's 'Some Principles of Film Restoration', *Griffithiana*, vol. 11 nos. 38–39, October 1990, pp. 170–3. Unfortunately, theoretical work on the analysis of silent cinema is still in a rudimentary phase. There are many suggestions on how to study individual films or groups of films, or for approaches to film production in the early days of cinema. However, there are as yet no books or essays which develop these ideas systematically. Among the exceptions to the rule is Roland Cosandey, *Film um 1910: Aus der Sammlung Joseph Joye (London)* (Basle: Stadtkino Basel, and Frankfurt-am-Main: Stroemfeld Verlag, 1993).

A preliminary, symptomatic understanding of the relationship between technology and style in the cinema, and of its implications for the study of silent film, can be obtained by comparing the contrasting opinions of David Bordwell, Janet Staiger and Kristin Thompson in *The Classical Hollywood Cinema*, with those of Barry Salt in *Film Style & Technology: History and Analysis*. For an outline of the main tendencies prevailing in institutions of higher education in the 1980s, see Thomas Elsaesser (ed.), *Early Cinema: Space, Frame, Narrative* (London: British Film Institute, 1990), which includes a full critical bibliography and comes with two film collections on VHS videotapes compiled by the National Film and Television Archive, London (*Early Cinema: Primitives and Pioneers*, 70' and 95'); Noël Burch, *Life to Those Shadows* (Berkeley: University of California Press, 1990); Tom Gunning, 'The Cinema of Attraction: Early Film, Its Spectator and the Avant-Garde', *Wide Angle*, vol. 8 nos. 3–4, 1986, pp. 63–70; André Gaudreault, *Du littéraire au filmique: Système du récit* (Paris: Méridien Klincksieck, 1988); Heide Schlüpmann, *Unheimlichkeit des Blicks: Das Drama des frühen deutschen Kino* (Basle: Roter Stern, and Frankfurt-am-Main: Stroemfeld Verlag, 1990); Fritz Güttinger, *Der Stummfilm im Zitat der Zeit* (Frankfurt-am-Main: Deutsches Filmmuseum, 1984); John L. Fell, *Film Before Griffith*; Miriam Hansen, *Babel and Babylon: Spectatorship in American Silent Film* (Cambridge, Mass.: Harvard University Press, 1991); *Early Cinema: From Origins to 1913* (special issue of *Persistence of Vision*, no. 9, 1991).

Regarding the problem of reproducing films on other media, see Dimitri Balachoff, 'Psycho-Physiology of Film and Video', *Bulletin de la Fédération Internationale des Archives de la Télévision/ International Federation of Television Archives Newsletter*, Special Issue, nos. 7–12, January 1986, reprinted in *The Perfect Vision*, vol. 2 no. 5, Fall 1989; John Belton, 'Pan and Scan Scandal', *The Perfect Vision*, vol. 1 no. 3, Indian Summer 1987, and 'The Shape of Money', *Sight and Sound*, vol. 57 no. 1, Winter 1987–88; Paolo Cherchi Usai, 'The Unfortunate Spectator', *Sight and Sound*, vol. 56 no. 3, Summer 1987, pp. 170–5; Tom Mann, 'High Definition Television as It Stands Today', *The BKSTS Journal*, September 1981; Harry Mathias and Richard Patterson, *Electronic Cinematography: Achieving Photographic Control Over the Video Image* (Belmont, Calif.: Wadsworth, 1985); Timothy Palmer-Benson, 'What's Wrong With Video', *The Perfect Vision*, vol. 1 no. 1, Winter 1986–87.

The consequences of using materials other than film in cinema studies are effectively summed up by the Society for Cinema Studies Task Force on Film Integrity (John Belton, Tom Doherty, Ellen Draper, Christine Holmlund and William Paul) in its 'Statement on the Use of Video in the Classroom', *Cinema Journal*, vol. 30 no. 4, Summer 1991, pp. 3–6 and by the contributions of Bill Nichols, Royal S. Brown and John Belton to this debate, published in the same journal, vol. 31 no. 4, Summer 1992, pp 60–72.

Rudolf Arnheim's remarks quoted on pp. 90 and 91 are from the foreword (pages ix, xi) to *New Essays on the Psychology of Art* (Berkeley: University of California Press, 1986).

* Publication details are given at a title's first mention only.